AND THE STARS FLEW WITH US

AND THE STARS FLEW WITH US

RANDY B. YOUNG

Copyright © 2022 by Randy B. Young

Cover and interior design: Robert Kern
Development editor: Leigh Lassiter
Copy editor: Grace Baker

Typeset in Arno Pro by TIPS Technical Publishing, Inc., Carrboro, NC

Produced and published in the United States of America

All rights reserved. No part of this book may be reproduced, scanned, or distributed in any printed or electronic form without permission from the author. The author can be contacted at randolphbyoung@gmail.com.

ISBN print: 978-1-890586-76-8
ISBN ebook: 978-1-890586-77-5

31 30 29 28 27 26 25 24 23 22   1 2 3 4 5

For Dad

Contents

Preface ix
Acknowledgments xxi

1.	North Carolina into Virginia	1
2.	Across the Appalachians	13
3.	Interstate 81 and Central Virginia	23
4.	Virginia into Pennsylvania	31
5.	Leaving Bellefonte	41
6.	Western Massachusetts	51
	Photo Insert	63
7.	Dartmouth and Northern New England	73
8.	I-91 South to Connecticut...	85
9.	Connecticut to New York City	97
10.	I-95 South to Maryland	105
11.	Southbound on I-85...	117

Epilogue 137
About the Author 145

Preface

> Every dreamer knows that it is entirely possible to be homesick for a place you've never been to, perhaps more homesick than for familiar ground.
> —Judith Thurman

American author Ernest Hemingway said that all true stories end in death. In many ways, this is a story that begins with one.

My father died in December 2017, a week shy of his ninetieth birthday. My brother Steve and I had been watching after both of my parents for some time by then, but I hadn't seen "Dad" in almost a decade. Not really.

He and my mother had been battling dementia for years and languishing in the memory care ward of a nearby assisted living center in Hillsborough, North Carolina, since 2015, just 10 miles from their home in Chapel Hill. They even shared a room. They spent the last days of their sixty-three-year marriage waking up each morning to a routine that was the same as the day before, yet strange and new. I wondered if they found consolation in that somewhat familiar smiling face across the room.

During their time there, Steve and I would visit from our own homes in nearby Chapel Hill and take them out regularly for rides through the countryside near their facility. For much of my parents' lives, Steve and I had been the passengers in the back seat. Dad—Maurice "Gus" Young—would usually be at the wheel, with Mom—Jackie Young—at his side. We had gone for countless family road trips and a million Sunday afternoon rides and laughed and loved and leaned into life as Dad told us stories that even he would find hard to believe later when we repeated them to him.

As I look back, many of my most vivid memories are framed through open car windows. I am both captivated and haunted by the road.

Dad's chosen career was in instruction. He taught junior high school physical education, coached junior high football, and coached high school track and field. Both Steve and I were lucky enough to have had him as a coach at one point or another—lucky enough to see him engaging in the most praiseworthy of professions: imparting knowledge and building confidence in impressionable young adults. He was a humble, caring man who sought out and championed the underdog, no doubt owing to his own youth. Abandoned by his parents by age three, he was remanded to his grandparents. He grew up poor, and he grew up late—at his high school graduation, he still looked like a sixth-grader.

Teaching is hard; Dad just made it look easy—he was a natural. And driving provided another teaching avenue for him. His chosen family car was a station wagon, and with windows all around, it was a moving classroom. If you wanted food for thought, our car was a 360-degree buffet.

To watch on from the backseat as my father set a course across New England backroads on Sunday rides or as he drove up and down I-95 to and from North Carolina was to see my father truly in his element. It was watching an artist create something beautiful: the ideal ride, the perfect family road trip (if there was one). As a child of the Great Depression, he wanted for a lot early in his life and was always conscious of cost. But driving was free.

I don't think Dad would have said his life began until he hit the open road in his late teens. He rode a lot of Greyhounds, but I'm not sure he ever drove a car until he was almost twenty, and that was in Mexico. Before he was done driving that first time, he'd violated any number of motor vehicle statutes and immigration laws.

My father may well have been an international refugee. The facts are hazy.

Following high school in Bellefonte, Pennsylvania, and an eighteen-month tour in the Marines, Dad headed west, as so many did in the late 1940s. Without a car, a license, or a plan, he took a bus to Los Angeles in December 1947. He never talked much about why he went or what he did there except to say that he stayed in a boarding house until his money ran out.

"I didn't know what I was doing," he said. "It was someplace different—anywhere different." Admittedly, there was hardly a place in the world more different from Bellefonte than L.A.

"Central Los Angeles had one tall building then, back before it got huge," he said. "Bellefonte had one small school."

After about two weeks, he packed his only suitcase again, and, without so much as a nickel for bus money, he prepared to hitchhike back east.

At the time, hitchhiking was considered safe and practical, if truly pedestrian. It was still steps above hopping boxcars like a hobo. He said he looked so rough that he probably caught rides out of sheer pity.

"I caught one ride with another ex-serviceman and his wife right out of L.A. They took me through the southwest, Texas, and all the way to the border of Louisiana. The next day, I stuck my thumb out and caught a ride all the way to Florida—Florida because it was still winter. I had an uncle from Bellefonte living there. I stayed with him for a night, and he showed me around some the next day—I saw my first orange grove—but he made it plain that he wasn't running a hotel.

"He loaned me a few dollars for food—not even enough for a bus ticket home," Dad said, "so it was back to hitchhiking again."

But it was only a couple of days out of California during an overnight stay near El Paso, Texas, that my father found himself in the driver's seat for the first time in his life.

"That first couple I was riding with wanted to cross the border for good tequila," Dad explained, "and they wanted me along. I'd already told them that I didn't drink, so having me as a back-up driver was probably part of their plan, though they hadn't told me anything about it."

The threesome headed into Juárez, Mexico, and found their way into a cantina.

"We spent hours in that Mexican bar," Dad said. The couple he was with spent the entire time getting drunk, leaving my father to fend off the advances of a remarkably plain Mexican woman. Apparently, she was "a regular" and was almost as sloshed as Dad's hosts.

"I just didn't want to be there," Dad said, "and, well, maybe she might have been attractive to someone as drunk as she was, but I wasn't."

On my wall today is a faded black-and-white photo taken in that cantina. It shows the drunk couple with a young guitarist standing behind them. On one side of the couple was a gaunt woman with buck teeth. Though much older than my father, her age did nothing to dissuade her amorous intentions for Dad. On the other side of the photo sat my young father, sober as a preacher, looking like he'd just been stranded on another planet.

It was late when they were finally ready for the hour-long drive back to El Paso. The car owner and his wife were good and drunk—certainly too drunk to drive or even navigate, and in 1948, that was saying something. Without the threat of breathalyzers or border law enforcement, prosecution of those "too drunk to drive" rarely occurred unless the drivers plowed through a booth at the border checkpoint.

I have also speculated that there may have been an illegal cache of contraband liquor in the trunk. My father's newfound hosts would have surely returned to the US with more tequila than they held in their belly, as impressive as that amount was.

Clearly, Dad was in the best condition to drive. His first time behind the wheel would be crossing the United States border at 3:00 a.m. with two drunks in the backseat and a distillery in the trunk. By the time they'd reached El Paso, Dad had driven in two countries without a driver's license, without experience, and without directions, likely violating any number of customs laws.

Dad didn't drive again for a year; he didn't visit Mexico again *ever*. For all we know, he's still a wanted man in Juárez.

Dad died on Christmas Eve. I wasn't with him when he passed, but he'd stopped eating a few weeks earlier, which often heralded a quick decline. I got the call at 7:30 a.m. that day in 2017 from a hospice nurse at the assisted living facility where he had been for nearly three years.

As I met the funeral home representatives in Mom and Dad's room and saw Dad into the hearse, my mother sat in the dining room cheerfully eating breakfast, surrounded by Christmas decorations and serenaded by carols. Mom was oblivious to all of it: the holidays, the strangers in her room, me, Dad. Dementia is undeniably cruel, but in rare twists of fate, it can also be merciful.

In the weeks that followed, Mom would occasionally ask where Gus was, but I would skirt the truth.

"I'm not sure . . . I haven't seen him."

She deserved honesty, but even when I was calmly direct with her, she could not truly grasp the truth of her new reality. She couldn't process it, but I could. It was just her now, *alone*.

Her demeanor remained unchanged through that holiday season. In early January 2018, we held a memorial service in the same church—in the same modest chapel, in fact—where Dad and Mom had been married sixty-three years before. Mom was there for the service, as were many of her old Chapel Hill girlfriends, though she didn't really recognize them.

Mom's decline would often lead her to be confused, forgetful, and nervous, but never given to anger, which was one of Dad's unfortunate symptoms. The disease would serve her well on this early January day, as the memorial was simply a church outing for her that she would forget by the end of the same day.

When the time came, I gave my father's eulogy, seasoning it with stories, insights, humor, and a celebration of that humility Dad so preciously and singularly espoused. The presentation was well-received, especially by the presiding minister, Reverend Mitch Simpson. After the service, Mitch *commanded* me to write. He said it was to honor my father, who he said would want me to write.

It was probably true. Dad was supportive of all my endeavors to a fault. If I drew a dinosaur in crayon in second grade, he would save the picture because it might portend a Nobel Prize in paleontology. The leap from "can do" to "should do professionally" was a short one for Dad, and I reveled in it.

Over time, I learned that my father was correct in the assessment of at least two talents: running and writing. I ran competitively in high school and college. I began to write shortly thereafter, first for fun and later to supplement the income at my day job.

When I wrote a weekly column in a local paper, Dad saved every article over decades. After he died, I discovered hundreds in a box in his office closet. So Reverend Mitch was probably right to issue his decree. Consequently, and with apologies to the Blues Brothers, at least one of the reasons I write these essays is because, apparently, I'm on a "mission from God."

There isn't one story that encapsulates my father's life, though there might be hundreds. If I didn't recognize them at the time, I do now. And so many of the venerated ones came of Dad's hands on a steering wheel with Mom at his side and Steve and I wrestling for space in the backseat.

Sure, there were Kodak moments and memories at home around a holiday hearth or watching Dad teach or coach. But many of my fondest memories of Dad were those fleeting moments of beauty on the road and the wonder found hidden in our sacred communion as the world rushed by us at sixty miles per hour.

As it happened, I'd already planned a trip to New England for the following summer of 2018. I would structure the trip around a few housekeeping elements: getting together with some high school buddies from around the area, paying a long-overdue visit with my best friend and fellow Dartmouth College alum Ted Fleming and his wife, Kathy, in central Connecticut, and then attending our college reunion together in Hanover, New Hampshire. But I would also spread some of Dad's cremated ashes in various spots along the route—appropriately in the places Dad might remember fondly and the places where he was remembered fondly.

For almost a decade, I'd looked straight into Dad's face and seen a poor stranger besieged by time, betrayed by his own mind and body, occasionally belligerent, and finally bedridden. But if I was truly looking for my father, I had to look elsewhere. So, as I took to the road that summer, I hoped that I might rediscover the "Dad" I had known at his most vital as opposed to the shell of the man I'd tended to over his final years. When I theoretically discovered my father again through stories from relatives in Pennsylvania where he'd grown up or through remembrances of former friends in

Massachusetts where we'd lived and he had worked, I knew I would grieve. But I also hoped to glean inspiration to write, as I'd been so "divinely charged."

Here is a tribute to my father or the road (if the two of them were separable), and to the elusive, mythical "Great American Road Trip." After all, videos fail, photos fade, memory corrupts, but literature just might endure beyond my father or me.

As a columnist covering local events, I had grown particularly fond of shining a light on personal triumphs over adversity—championing the underdog. And if there was an underdog, it was Dad.

Others have spoken and written eloquently and wisely about the human need to journey too. As words go, Steinbeck's are epic. Homer was mythic, Kerouac was rhythmic, and John Hughes was comic. But perhaps the truth lay in all four—the tragic, the beautiful, the hilarious, star-crossed, ugly, elegant truth.

So I took to the road myself that very June, with my father's urnful of ashes for a copilot and with no preconceived notion of what might happen. Whether Dad was steering a team of athletes, a classroom, or a car, he was a teacher. I wondered what lessons he had left to teach me even in death and this, our final collaboration. Here, then, is an homage to the open road and the belief that what's around the corner will be new and amazing—celebrating that certainty that a left turn toward God-knows-what is ultimately more wondrous than a right turn homeward. Framed in my own travels, what follows reflects both recent and long-held memories as a tribute to Dad, those who knew him, and the journey he held so dear.

Enjoy the ride.

> I find I'm so excited that I can barely sit
>   still or hold a thought in my head.
> I think it's the excitement only a free man
>   can feel.
> A free man at a start of a long journey
>   whose conclusion is uncertain.
>   —*Red, The Shawshank Redemption*

Acknowledgments

A heartfelt thank you...

To my wife, Kelly, for all of her support, love, and writing advice. Your navigational skills and your place beside me in the front seat are still central to our own family trips and so many of my most salient and cherished memories. May we always be side by side gazing out at the world in amazement.

To my own children, Alexa and Harrison, for sparing your father for so many hours at the computer writing. I may forever debate the perils of GPS mapping with you, but I only hope you experience the joy of having children such as yourselves with whom you enjoy the role of tour guide to the world.

To my brother, Steve, for enduring snippets and paragraphs I would read incessantly and for not correcting me every time he thought he remembered something differently (which was often). And to his wife, Lesley, who has always supported my writing and was the first person to read my previous novel, a laborious task to be sure.

To my mother (who died in early 2021), without whose navigational skills and patience, we'd probably still be lost in Wilmington, Delaware, and surviving on Beechnut Gum and Cheddar Cheez Nabs. I miss you, Mom.

For Ted and Kathy Fleming, who so often opened up their home and their hearts and are, in every sense of the word, family.

For Ron and Joyce Howard and my Bellefonte, Pennsylvania, family, for playing host for our get-togethers, for preserving memories of my parents so dearly, for slaving over pierogies, and for the advice I should have taken to stay away from the local abandoned quarry.

For all of the folks at TIPS Technical Publishing, including development editor Leigh Lassiter, for limiting the number of times I got tangled up in my own stories; copy editor Grace Baker; proofreader Emma Gerden; and publisher Robert Kern. Sometimes the best roads to travel start right in your own backyard.

And for Mitch and Betty Simpson, who loved and ministered to my parents, and who set me on a "mission from God."

1

North Carolina into Virginia

Out-and-Back, Dead Birds, and "Bum-Bum-Bo"

> Superstition is foolish, childish, primitive
>   and irrational—
> but how much does it cost you to knock
>   on wood?
>
> —Judith Viorst

The beginning of any truly great endeavor suggests a moment of glorious terror . . . maybe a few.

For example, when I waited at the starting line of my first marathon, I couldn't help but panic. *Where am I? How the hell did I get here? Whose idea was this anyway? Can I still get out of it?* Incidentally, I was still asking myself these same things twenty-three miles into the race.

At 11:00 a.m. on a Saturday in late June 2018, I sat in my driveway, ready to embark on a drive from Chapel Hill, North Carolina, to New England and back. Fumbling nervously with the keys to my Subaru Outback, I thought, *Whose idea was this? I wonder if I can still get out of it.*

I'd been here before. A measure of panic just meant that I was doing it right. I was not one to take an endeavor of any magnitude lightly, and I knew deep down that I was prepared, that I'd ticked all the boxes.

I'd said goodbye to my son, Harrison, the night before, as he was heading out of town for a long weekend. I'd shared a quiet morning with my wife, Kelly, and given goodbye kisses to her and my daughter, Alexa. Both now stood in the driveway to see me off.

I'd been on dozens of road trips with my familial traveling companions, but my son was taking summer courses at the University of North Carolina, and my daughter was working. My wife was also unable to make the trip due to work. On the one hand, there was nobody's schedule to meet but my own, nobody to insist on visits to rest stops every mile, and nobody to roll their eyes when I missed an exit or blew past a stop sign. On the downside, this meant that there would be nobody to laugh or cry or share experiences with. There was no one to confer with on directions or traffic. This trip and the search to rediscover and reclaim Dad six months after his passing were mine and mine alone, and no roadmap would point the way. Still . . .

"I can't help but think I'm forgetting something," I told my wife.

"I don't see how," Kelly said dryly. "You've got the whole house in your car."

Everything had been packed and loaded, just so, into the car, from the trivial to the crucial, and I'd always prided myself on that exercise in geometry that is the perfectly packed car. In the rear seat were the things I might need along the way—things I could reach for without taking my eyes off the road: a camera, drinks and snacks from a cooler, and a sweatshirt in case it grew chillier, which it was bound to do at some point during this trip northward. In the front, I had more snacks, a notebook with plans and reservations, multiple pairs of sunglasses, a notepad, my iPhone, a giant cup of hot coffee, and one hospital-grade HealthyKin male portable plastic urinal "with a handy angled design and EZ-grip contoured handle."*

*The use of one of these items while driving would go catastrophically wrong, but more on that later.

And then there was Dad. Coach Maurice E. "Gus" Young sat in my copilot's seat riding shotgun. The master of all road trips I'd ever either enjoyed or endured in my youth was still by my side in a Carolina-blue urn, securely belted into the passenger seat. I'd placed Dad's old Carolina baseball cap on top of his urn, and a coach's whistle hung by a shoestring around the neck where it narrowed. This assortment of keepsakes reminded me of Dad more than any manifestation I'd seen for years.

The urn was inviolable; it was not to be opened. Alternatively, a cylindrical cardboard dispenser was next to the urn and filled with the ashes I would spread. With this, I hoped to get to know Dad again—the man who, in his final few years, had disappeared into a maelstrom of antipsychotics, confusion, and fear. Aside from being grandly decorated with snow-capped Rocky Mountain vistas, the dispenser was cardboard, functional at best, and resembled a can of Comet Bath and Tile Cleaner.

I still felt something gnawing at me—something I'd forgotten. What if the car doesn't start? Now that would be a sure sign to reconsider this quixotic quest, a missing-person search for someone who was no longer there. I stabbed the key into the ignition, and it turned over eagerly. I smiled at Kelly and gave a thumbs-up.

"Oh yes," she said. "Bravo. Well done. Now go, have a great time, and call later. I love you."

"Love you too," I said. Backing out of the driveway, I took a long look at my wife's and daughter's faces. "I'll be right back."

In the grand scope, this was true. I would return to the very same driveway in just over a week as if nothing had happened. But if nothing else moved an inch and the grass stopped growing and the world stopped turning, *I* would still have changed. If we travel a million miles to arrive at the point of origin, the miles themselves change us. We are far different people returning from our adventures than those who left. We are richer.

I'd interviewed author and ultrarunner Dean Karnazes for an installment of the weekly sports column I wrote for a time. I asked him what his plans were *after* running. He explained that he would simply keep going until he could run no farther.

"Life is *not* an out-and-back," he said confidently.

But sometimes it is, I now understand. Dad ended his life in a childlike state, timid, reactive, and dependent on others. But an out-and-back doesn't mean nothing changes. I knew in my heart that there was an infinitely wise and gentle man somewhere hidden beneath the facade, who had seen more and done more than I could imagine—who was somehow greater for the journey, even if I couldn't always see it.

Our life itself *is* an out-and-back, and it is filled with a succession of out-and-backs in ever-widening circles. Sometimes, adventure is just one lap around the track . . . or several. Maybe it's a day, maybe it's a lifetime, and maybe it's both. It's in the fabric of the universe, from the very large to the very small. It's in the orbit of the planets, the music of the spheres, the generations of families, and the course of our own lives.

I could do this. Here was just another wondrous lap that might change me in ways I could not yet know.

I turned southbound along the divided NC-86 for about 200 yards before pulling a U-turn and heading north past the house, giving a last somber wave to my wife and daughter. Missing them already, I turned to Dad for consolation, but there was none to be given, and I found myself tearing up.

"Shit," I thought. "I'm already emotional, and I haven't even gotten past the Food Lion."

Across I-40 and through Hillsborough, North Carolina, I traversed familiar roads where I'd taken my parents on so many brief escapes from assisted living. North of Hillsborough, however, I embarked on a new landscape. Businesses grew scarcer. Wild roses, Muscadine grapes, and blankets of kudzu retreated from the roadsides, and any hills flattened out into ancient family farmlands.

I hadn't felt this alone and far from home for some time, and that feeling of panic descended all over again.

Dad killed a bird. There it is.

I'm not sure where or when—maybe around 1968?—but by the way it was lodged into the grill of our light blue 1965 Dodge Dart station wagon, it hit us at seventy miles per hour. More if it had been flying toward us.

It wasn't big or particularly colorful. I believe it was probably a wren or a chickadee—we didn't even notice it until there was really no telling. By the time we were curious, it really was just a beak and lump of feathers. When we asked Dad what kind of bird it was, he said, "A lucky one." Dad thought a moment and reconsidered. "Well, not so lucky for the bird, but good luck for us."

This may or may not have been true, but it didn't matter. He *said* it was. If I'd learned anything from Dad's parenting, coaching, or driving, it was this: it was far more important to be *sure* than to be *right*. Dad was more boldly confident about sketchy, inessential information than anyone I knew. It served him well, but I think we as children also preferred it. If he was wrong, it would usually be forgotten the next minute; if he was right, his surety appeared mystical.

"Why is the sky blue?" we'd ask.

"Because God's a Carolina Tar Heels fan," he'd reply, without missing a beat. And we would believe him.

And watching sports highlights on TV, Dad would often predict what was shown:

"Hey, watch this sixty-foot putt," he would say. "I'll bet it goes in." He was always right, and it never occurred to us that, if it didn't go in, it would not have been a televised highlight.

So, when he said that the dead bird was a "lucky bird," we took it as gospel. God was a Tar Heels fan, and this bird had blessed the station wagon. What more did we need?

There was the magic to that, I think. Even just the façade of absolute knowledge—a confident fiction—was preferable to an ambiguous truth. So we never asked why he considered the dead bird "lucky." He joked flippantly that it might be a stern warning to other birds to steer clear. More likely, it was simply too gross a chore to remove. After all, it was stuck fast, as if welded into place. Dad refused to scrape or dig the damned thing out. The creature stayed there for three years—until we sold the car.

Or maybe killing the bird was poetically unlucky, and Dad wasn't letting on. As he took the wheel and sailed down America's roads, perhaps he felt he'd killed a figurative albatross, and this was his penance. In the "Rime of the Ancient Mariner" by Coleridge, a sailor who killed the bird was forced to wear it around his neck. Dad was just wearing it in our grill.

I believe Dad was, on balance, more superstitious than he would let on. He would have fit in well among mariners, who had all kinds of unsupported beliefs about what brought on good or bad luck. Fridays and Candlemas were considered horrible days to set sail, for example. The sirens of myth were always a danger, as sirens certainly were on any modern road trip, so best to steer clear of those as well. Whistling brought bad fortune to a boat, as it was said to mock the wind and weather. Bananas were bad luck. I've no clue what was going on there. I'm not sure I want to know.

Dad simply couldn't whistle, so no trouble there; he rarely sped, so we were rarely confronted with sirens. At the end of the day, he was about ritual. As a football and track coach, he would never allow any of his players to curse or spit on the field or track, as these were sacred arenas—like churches. As a University of North Carolina alum, he would never think of jinxing a UNC basketball team. If the Tar Heels were up by forty points, it was "time to bear down"; if we were down twenty points with seconds to go, he would assure everyone in the room that "*Now* we got 'em just where we want 'em."

And he had one necessary preface to any family trip: a ritual rally cry. I first heard my father utter it as we began a road trip to Colorado in 1966. It was probably a simple chant he'd heard from cheerleaders at UNC football games, but it eventually served as a christening of all road trips. Each time we hit the highway as a family thereafter, he'd shout it and we'd all chime in:

"*Bum-bum-bo, here we go.*" That set us on our way. "*Bum-bum-bum, here we come,*" signaled our return. Out and back.

Silly, I know. I'm not saying it guaranteed safe travels. We simply weren't willing to test the theory. I've taken to shouting it at the start of my own family's road trips nowadays. It seems that there are neither atheists in foxholes nor fatalists in heavy traffic.

By 1:00 p.m., I had approached the Virginia state line and the southeastern foothills of the Appalachians were mounting up under the road bit by bit, like a rising tide. Each hill was a higher cresting wave, topped with large billboards, steeples that seemed to stretch up to heaven, and congregations of rusted cars and tractors. Adrift on seas of kudzu and corn, I was lulled by the visual white noise of passing roadside open-air garden centers, "Kutesie Kurl" hair salons, home-cured jerky, and Circle K "fresh" pizza signs. Roadkill dotted the pavement, and pirate flags of the Confederacy loomed menacingly.

Rough seas.

I'd often wondered if, in an earlier life, I'd been some sea-going drifter, steered by the stars or the winds. Or perhaps at the helm of my own vessel. There's something in my soul that seems to awaken at the sound of a gull's cry, and it has often resonated on long stretches of straight road. A mariner's refrain from John Masefield's poem "Sea Fever" sang to me as I prepared to swing around the Danville bypass on a port tack:

> I must go down to the seas again, to the lonely sea
>   and the sky,
> And the wheel's kick and the wind's song and white
>   clouds flying . . .
> . . . Is a wild call and a clear call that may not
>   be denied;

> . . . And all I ask is a merry yarn from a laughing fellow-rover,
> And quiet sleep and a sweet dream when the long trick's over.

After passing north of a remarkably un-scenic tour of historic downtown Lynchburg, Virginia, I took a left turn off Route 29 in Amherst, which sent me hurtling westward toward the spine of the Blue Ridge Mountains, Buena Vista below the western slope, and I-81 North. That interstate would deliver me to my night one destination in Hagerstown, Maryland. From there, I'd travel to my father's hometown in central Pennsylvania, farther northward to Massachusetts where my father had taught and coached and where I'd grown up, and finally to Hanover, New Hampshire, with my friend Ted Fleming for my Dartmouth College thirty-five-year reunion.

This day already felt like it was comprised of a dozen trips. The best day trips are like that. Every grand bit of circulation is a series of smaller ones. Any great journey is a series of shorter tours. The best adventures hold within them a small eternity.

After hours beneath a regatta of white puffy clouds, the turn west from Amherst gave the first glimpse of real weather and thin rows of passing showers. They poured intermittently on Route 60 as I headed toward the leading edge of the Appalachians and rode the troughs and furrows of the front range. Diving deep into valleys where the air itself was pregnant with squalls felt like drowning in the murky, deep end of a pool.

In a clearing, I could see a half-dozen showers around me punctuated by sunlit fields before a final ascent and crossing beneath the Blue Ridge Parkway overpass. Rising out of the depths, a ray of sun struck the Carolina blue of the urn and it occurred to me: I realized what I'd forgotten.

"Bum-bum-bo..." I said under my breath, to no one, really. "Here we go..."

Now, I was on my way. *Now*, it was a road trip.

2

Across the Appalachians

Somewhere over the Parkway, Color TVs, and Time Travel

> Watch with glittering eyes the whole world around you because the greatest secrets are always hidden in the most unlikely places.
> Those who don't believe in magic will never find it.
>
> —*Roald Dahl*

Strange things have been witnessed in the Appalachians. The Bell Witch and Mothman. Brown Mountain Lights. The Flatwood Monster. And yes, I'll say it: *time travel*.

The showers broke and the sun returned as I crested the 500-million-year-old Appalachian ridge, slipped under a Blue Ridge Parkway overpass, and rode the waterslide down toward Buena Vista, which sat at the very foot of the Eastern Continental Divide (waters to the west ultimately flowed into the Mississippi River; waters to the east flowed into the

Atlantic Ocean). The town was fed by the Maury River and once provided commerce with the outside world by the Richmond and Alleghany Railroad and the Shenandoah Valley Railroad. It was famous for Southern Virginia University and frequent floods, though apparently not for a flood of population and tourism.

This was to be only my second time in Buena Vista. I'd aged forty-eight years since my first visit. I wondered if the town had aged as well. I wondered if my descent from the Eastern Continental Divide would send me cascading back in time as it had done decades ago. Maybe it would send me back even further.

It was in July 1970, on a family trip from Massachusetts to our mom's mother, Luna Crawford, in Chapel Hill, North Carolina, when we went back in time. It was a Tuesday.

I was nine years old; my brother, Steve, was five. Sometimes we made the same north-south pilgrimage via I-95 with its city traffic, detours, and innumerable bypasses. When we made a pitstop in central Pennsylvania to visit my father's relatives, we would opt for an inland route which was less direct and hillier but far less stressful. Given the season, we'd chosen to avoid the heat at lower elevations by heading south along the Blue Ridge Parkway in Virginia, which cut a swath through Shenandoah National Park and tight-roped the crest of the Blue Ridge Mountains.

There weren't restaurants or stores, and service stations only popped up every thirty miles or so. As it was a weekday, there wasn't even that much traffic. We might have been the only people alive save for passengers in the rare cars we saw passing in the opposite direction.

As we rocketed through dense pockets of clouds that drifted across the road at three thousand feet, it was dreamlike . . . otherworldly. My brother and I sat in the backseat, whining about when we might stop for a soda, a candy bar, or anything other than the snacks Mom had kept in her purse since the Eisenhower administration.

We'd been on the Parkway all afternoon, forestalling as long as possible the dive down into heat and humidity for dinner and a place to stay. My mom was looking over the map; Dad navigated the turns in the wandering mists, out of which RVs and Airstreams would seem to materialize before us.

"Buena Vista," Mom said. "There's probably a hotel in Buena Vista, right, Gus?"

Dad threw a quick glance at the map and Mom pointed at some dot amidst the meaningless, colorful lines.

"Look for Route 60 coming up," Mom said.

"We want a pool . . ." Steve chirped.

"—and a color TV," I added.

This was all that was important to Steve and me. Our television at home was a black-and-white Zenith. Color television was everything. We could stand transfixed before a console color TV on display at some Sears watching a weather forecast and looking like we'd just landed in Oz with all its sudden, colorful splendor. Mom could shop for hours, and it didn't matter. We stayed rooted to the spot, watching *The Wild Wild West* or *Star Trek*.

"Wait, Spock's shirt is blue?" *Who knew?*

(For those born after 1970, I want to share that parents once regularly left kids alone in stores and on playgrounds without worry. They also sent children to school with Marshmallow Fluffernutter sandwiches for a nutritious lunch. Admittedly, however, these were often the same children that burned bugs with magnifying glasses for fun.)

Swimming was another luxury. We rarely swam in Massachusetts. Pools near our house were above-ground, and they were insufferably cold. A warm pool and a color TV: these were our demands. Dinner didn't even make the list.

As we turned west onto Route 60 and sank below the underbelly of the clouds, the heat and humidity weighed down. The temperature rose about thirty degrees over the span of our four-minute plunge into Buena Vista.

Stranger still, the town was a picture postcard from the 1930s. Everywhere we looked, there were old cars. Cadillac V-16s and Roadsters, Model A Fords, Brewster town cars, Buicks: all pristine, all cruising up and down the main boulevard.

Nobody said a word. However, we all thought it. We were all aware that we'd been in a place out of time all day and that we'd seemed to have tumbled into the "Town that Time Forgot." The possibility that we'd lurched back about forty years over the course of our afternoon seemed more interesting than some plausible explanation like an antique car show or some town event. And after all, didn't Buena Vista sound like the town name from a Twilight Zone episode?

Mom looked at Dad, but he just gazed about, unfazed. Finally, my brother Steve spoke up.

"Can the old-time people *see* us?"

It was a valid question. There was not a Toyota Corona or a Honda to be found. I thought it reassuring when our car's reflection appeared in a store window—we were indeed visible. I wondered if our presence astounded the 1930s population we'd encountered, the way the Starship Enterprise might have caused a stir if it landed in Yankee Stadium.

We ended up at a hotel that was a couple of dollars more per night but met the demands of the emotional hostage crisis we'd imposed on our parents: air conditioning, a pool, and a color TV. The pool was cold, but we would have swum in the Bering Sea. Any swim was a luxury, and just on principle, we were going to get our money's worth.

By the time we returned to the room, Dad had picked up pizza. Mom was busying herself apportioning the dinner, paper plates, and napkins, Steve and I showered, and Dad tried to understand TV dials which were strange and new to him.

"What the heck is 'tint'?" he said, fumbling with a knob until the whole screen turned greenish. "Oh, *that's* 'tint.'" Still damp from the showers, Steve and I bounced on the hotel beds in our pajamas, hollering approval for the green screen, if only because it wasn't *gray*.

Dad spent about fifteen minutes adjusting the colors and reception with the rabbit-ear antenna that shot up from behind the set. He found three channels that offered any reception in the low valley. On one was an episode of *Lassie*, but *in black and white*. A second channel had signed off for the night—at 8:00 p.m. no less—but the color test pattern was undeniably beautiful. This channel was our fallback position.

Finally, Dad found the Major League Baseball All-Star Game dressed in all its colorful finery. "Ahhh," he said, stepping back and folding his arms. "This will do fine."

I've no memory of where the game was played or who won, but I can remember to this day the colorful uniforms and the red, white, and blue banners draped everywhere around the stadium.

This was magical, by our reckoning. Some would say it wasn't, of course. They'd similarly argue that birds in the grill don't really ensure good fortune. They'd say that changes in altitude don't turn back time. I just preferred a world in which they *did*.

I sometimes wonder if the mysteries of life—tales of monsters and myths—aren't better left that way. There are times when the enchanted explanations are far preferable to the real and empirical, especially during childhood. Kids ask a lot of questions when they don't want the real answers. Sometimes a quick, confident, and creative fib is so much more fitting and fun.

From where I sit, magic *is* possible, and Santa is real (I'll leave cookies and milk for him 'til my dying day, even if I end up eating them). Good luck charms and incantations are essential, a color television and a pool are rare treasures indeed, and entire towns can be lost in time. That's the world I prefer to live in, and I feel closer to it on the road than just about anywhere else in the universe . . . or any *time*. I hope I always will—if I ever *stop* believing, shame on me.

As I continued through 2018 Buena Vista, I counted any number of walk-in hotels which might have been where we stayed nearly fifty years prior. I tried to absorb as much from this mysterious place as I could on my way to somewhere else. That might have been the town's credo: "Buena Vista, Virginia: A nice town on the way to somewhere else."

It didn't seem like 2018 there, but it also wasn't stuck in the 1930s anymore. Storefronts were as they might have appeared in the early 1970s or 1980s. The hotels still had "Heated Pool" and "Color TVs" flickering on their marquees, as if these reflected extravagances over other hotels down the road. I wouldn't have been surprised to see painted on a store window: "Yes, we have digital watches, VHS tapes, and Sony Walkmans!"

Maybe we'd been mistaken on our first visit. Traversing the entire town of some six square miles in roughly forty-five seconds, my fleeting and possibly unfair impression was that maybe the town wasn't mired in the early twentieth century after all. Perhaps it was just trailing the rest of the world by forty years, happily keeping pace at the back of the pack. I found this both sad and merciful. True, the population probably had to hear of Elvis's death, but it also probably didn't concern itself with TikTok posts or Kanye West's political leanings.

Still, seeing my first signs for I-81 to the west, I already felt nostalgic. I feel that way leaving any town behind. Passing through such a place was like passing through life. It would go on there long after I left—long after I moved on. Flowers would bloom, little triumphs and tragedies would play themselves out, and other visitors would come and go. There is both terror and peace in knowing that, when I'm gone, the world will do just fine without me.

As I passed the last storefront on the road through town, I looked for the reflection of my Subaru Outback in a large window as I passed, and, for just a moment, I could swear I saw our old Dodge with Dad at the wheel, smiling confidently.

And now, seeing Buena Vista as an adult—with that vantage from behind the curtain hung by the conspiracy of age and objectivity and cynicism—it still proved what a wizard my father had been. Without really trying, from his humble place behind the wheel one steamy day in 1970, he'd transformed *this* town into a place that, if not magical, was undeniably memorable. Dad had provided us with a color TV, a swim, and a story that now outlived him.

Now *that's* magic.

3

Interstate 81 and Central Virginia

Trucks, Rainbows, and Flying Stars

> When we contemplate the whole globe as one great dewdrop, striped and dotted with continents and islands, flying through space with other stars all singing and shining together as one, the whole universe appears as an infinite storm of beauty.
>
> —*John Muir*

To travel north on Interstate 81 is to walk in ancient footsteps.

The highway runs along the floor of a valley between two of the ridges of the Blue Ridge Mountains. It heads northeast from Tennessee to Canada, following the Appalachian chain through five US states along the same route as ancient animal migrations and, later, the Native Americans who hunted them. American settlers and Civil War troops also found this to be the path of least geographical resistance. Now it serves as a trucking corridor, often used as an alternative to the busier I-95 to the east.

Oh yeah, that's right: *trucks*. I'd almost forgotten about trucks. As I mounted the on-ramp to Interstate 81 North just west of Buena Vista, I realized that my journey had been mercifully free of their Jurassic gait since setting out.

Also, billboards: there *they* were. Litter too. And exit markers for McDonald's, Waffle Houses, and truck stops where the same hotdogs had rolled on greasy grills for years and where mummified burritos awaited.

Northbound, I could look to the west out of my window and see the rolling hills of the George Washington and Jefferson National Forests. To my right were the ridges of Shenandoah National Park. Cars flew along the valley like bobsleds. Southbound lanes led past Buena Vista toward Roanoke, but in front of me was Harrisonburg, Virginia, then West Virginia, Maryland, and a wall of angry-looking clouds.

When I slammed into the rain, visibility dropped to around fifty feet. It was a terrible way to travel at seventy miles per hour but a great way to make time, because it frightened many of the timid drivers into break-down lanes or shelter beneath overpasses. I splashed past arrogant eighteen-wheelers to whom I'd sworn many a vendetta over the past one hundred miles.

I pushed through the torrents, the sky finally brightened, and the landscape widened. Draped just above the mountains and rain-soaked railroad yards at their feet, the sun painted a rainbow out the passenger-side windows. If I took a right turn at an off-ramp, I could drive right under it. The exits flew by, but that glorious sight accompanied me for an hour, mirroring my every mile.

I took it as an omen. Every long trip deserves at least a few, but you must be on the watch for them. They're *not* always right in front of you, and we too often ignore the ones that are.

We don't look around much anymore.

From our living rooms to our workstations, everything deemed important is strategically thrust right before our eyes; everything else is merely a distraction. We seek companionship on tiny smartphones and deftly "swipe right" or "swipe left," saving some options for later or dismissing others entirely. The term "head-turner" has no meaning anymore.

It's not that different from the driver's seat, where we're often focused solely on the destination before us, intent only on making time.

Being predators, our human eyes stare straight ahead (most prey have eyes to either side—try sneaking up on a housefly). Drivers stalk the roads and highways, competing for lanes, for speed. Passing a slow-moving vehicle is a personal victory; being stuck behind a slow one is infuriating. Anyone with a turn signal on for no apparent reason is to be separated from the herd and eaten. It's just natural selection.

It's different from the rear seat. There, you are free to stare out at the world. For rear passengers, it's an ever-evolving landscape in every direction, constantly changing and infinitely diverse. With all that beauty around us, my brother and I were not the kind to sit back quietly on trips or rides.

When we were young, children weren't chained down by seatbelts, and backseat windows could be rolled all the way down. While we occasionally fought over that small sliver of precious space between the front headrests and a seat at the grown-ups' table, we'd just as often roll down our windows and tilt our heads out into the breeze. Perched like Labrador retrievers with our chins on our forearms, we gulped mouthfuls of air and slipped into sleep as the wind roared in our ears.

After sundown, highways offered the opportunity for fantasy—a glance into other cars as we passed or ones that zoomed by. One might suppose a lot peeking into fellow travelers' private lives like that, even if it was dimly lit by a dome light or the dashboard, but the glimpse was fleeting and felt like an invasion of others' sanctums.

During this prehistory, station wagons' rear seats offered a reclined rest on overnight trips. Once the sun went down and they'd stuffed us with fast food, Mom and Dad would fold the back seat down and lay out a soft pad and blankets for a pallet. Steve and I would even change into pajamas.

We could no longer sit properly because the folded back seat added height. We would have to tilt our heads to lean over the front seat before we finally resigned ourselves to sleep. The shift from seats to bedding was a commitment to the night.

Eventually, we'd lay back with our feet forward and pull one of Dad's itchy military blankets up around us. From there, we were a million miles from our parents' conversations, which rose and fell. Talk radio on low-watt AM stations, one after another, ground into static every few miles, and we were serenaded by the lullaby of our tires. If a window was open, there was an aroma of the highway—that mix of fast food, exhaust, and sweet, wild grasses—which mixed and mingled with the smell of our parents' coffees. Neither my brother nor I ever wanted to nod off first. We would fight it. We reclined in the dark and talked of nothing, giggled at everything, and drew silly pictures in the air.

Around 1971, we traded our 1965 Dodge Dart for the smooth contours of a 1972 model year Dodge Coronet Custom station wagon. This was life changing.

It was mustard yellow, which Dad hated. We might have waited for one in sky-blue, but they were in high demand, our Dart was getting older, and Steve and I were growing—we needed more room. More importantly, the Coronet came with organized compartments—small pockets molded into the interior walls—where we could store anything from flashlights to snacks. And we never cleaned them out. By the time my parents sold that car around 1980, each compartment held strange wonders dating to the Nixon administration: unfinished Tootsie Pops, melted gum, random playing cards, a sticky pair of dice.

The Coronet was also much more aerodynamic than the Dart. All windows sloped inward at the top, for example. Dad hated this because leaving windows open even the slightest bit might allow rain to seep in. But it also meant that the wagon's rear window sloped forward. This allowed Steve and me to lay back on our pallet with rolled-up sweatshirts for pillows and gaze straight up through the rear window at the sky as we hurtled through the night.

Dawn was undeniable when it finally came. Light poured in from every window, and my brother and I would resist it until we finally stirred and groggily begged for breakfast.

But through the deep of night, everywhere was inky blackness where distant front porch lights or small town streetlights would occasionally streak by like shooting stars. The glow of distant cities would cast silos and steeples in ghostly silhouettes. But above us, through the glass and into the depth of night, the stars hung motionless out in all that cold.

A single mile or a thousand would not change our perspective on the universe. But for a few moments on the dreamy edge of sleep, there was a sense that the stars were along for the ride. We couldn't outrun them if we wanted to. They flew with us as surely as if they knew the way. For all our speed, the constellations would not come unhinged.

All was right in the heavens, and we fell asleep bundled up warm and safe in that confidence.

I pulled off I-81 into northern Hagerstown, Maryland, at 7:30 p.m. and wound around endless service roads until I found the hotel where I had reservations. Later that night, after a dinner of Maryland crab cakes, I returned to my hotel room. Eventually shutting off the television, I lay in the dark for a good bit with my father's urn and ashes on the bedside table. Say what you will about our obsession with mortal remains, I would not leave Dad all alone in a hotel parking lot.

Even so, I suddenly felt very much alone. I missed my wife and grown children and my dog, I missed my cat (and that's *saying* something), and I missed the Andromeda Galaxy on the bathroom nightlight. I missed my own bed.

Staring up from my pillow after a full day's travel, I could still smell the highway, and the roar of the road still rang in my ears. I recalled dreaming in the back of a station wagon on a dark stretch of highway, unfettered by the weight of worry and as light as the ether.

But my God, how I missed my precious stars.

4

Virginia into Pennsylvania

Stadiums, Dinosaurs, and Going the Extra Mile

> I may not have gone where I intended to go, but I think I have ended up where I needed to be.
> —*Douglas Adams*

There is rain, and that's fine. Then there are days when inescapable gloom seeps into every nook and cranny.

Sunday morning broke gray and dreary and would stay that way. Waves of low clouds rolled across the pastures just south of the Pennsylvania border. I-81 continued northward toward Harrisburg, but I plotted a stealthier route west of Chambersburg, where satellite dishes dotted the farms and fields like wildflowers.

Towns like Shade Gap, Breezewood, and Burnt Cabins, Pennsylvania, passed without so much as a stop sign. Weathered, bronze plaques boasted how the towns had once been home to US senators, governors, or presidents. The occasional general stores offered outlandishly expensive gasoline, lotto tickets, and homemade jerky. When customers walked by on creaky wooden floors, pickled eggs jiggled in their tall jars by the cash registers.

The tall, rain-soaked grasses that skirted the foothills of the Rothrock and Bald Eagle State Forests were lush and dense. Roadside streams were swollen and angry and moved almost as fast as the traffic.

As rich and beautiful as these winding roads were, I longed for a mileage marker to provide a sense of progress. Then came the first faded sign for Penn State University Football, out of date, likely forsaken in the wake of coach Joe Paterno's fall from favor a few years prior. Penn State University didn't announce itself until roads descended out of the hills into tree-lined lanes and faculty homes in State College, PA.

The goal was to make it to see my father's family near Bellefonte, Pennsylvania, for dinner, only eight miles to the north. But for the first time, I felt my father's insistence from the seat beside me, compelling me to take a short detour to see the campus and visit the football stadium.

Dad never felt like he'd been *anywhere* unless he'd seen the local football stadium. He would drive well out of the way on his quest to see it, even if only from the outside. It was important and memorable to us because it was important and memorable to *him*, however casually he played it off.

"See that stadium?" Dad would say, pointing across highway lanes and a wide slice of Baltimore or Pittsburg or Washington, DC. "That's where Johnny Unitas (or Bobby Lane or Sonny Jurgensen) played."

I remember the passing sight of NFL stadiums from Arrowhead in Kansas City or Mile High in Denver to Candlestick in San Francisco and grew to know the ghosts that haunted them. There was a huge arrowhead in front of the Kansas City Chiefs' stadium, but that was about all you could see from I-70. My earliest memory of Mile High Stadium in Denver was the misconception that the stadium itself stretched a mile high from the playing field to the upper decks. (The name, of course, refers to Denver's high elevation.)

The only professional stadium we'd seen the inside of was an old stadium below the elevated highway in Hartford, Connecticut, where Dad would explain that the semi-pro Hartford Knights once played. He pointed that out at least a hundred times.

But Dad never actually entered a professional football stadium. We went to see the New England Patriots' training camp at the University of Massachusetts–Amherst once and watched a preseason practice, but only because it didn't cost anything.

"It's cheaper from our living room," Dad would rationalize. "Plus, I already have a parking spot, the food's free, and the bathroom lines are shorter." He did take us to a couple Red Sox games in Boston's Fenway Park, but only because the bleacher seats were seven dollars then. I still haven't entered a professional football stadium to this day.

By Dad's reckoning, pro football arenas were hallowed ground, as sure as if they were the great churches of Europe (and these *secular* cathedrals were certainly liable to see bigger crowds on Sundays). He visited college stadiums, too, which led him to attend college itself.

After serving in the Marines and his short trip to California (and Mexico), he found himself searching for a direction. While visiting North Carolina in the summer of 1948 to see a girl, he ventured into Chapel Hill and visited a football practice at the University of North Carolina. After a session, he even introduced himself to Coach Carl Snavely, who had coached a year or two in Bellefonte after Dad left town. Snavely inquired as to Dad's thoughts on a potential UNC recruit who was just graduating high school there.

"Is he any good?" Snavely asked.

"Well, he's not that talented," said Dad, trying to be diplomatic, "but he *is* pretty."

Seeing that Dad was in shape, needing to fill out the roster, and knowing my father was on the G.I. Bill and would not cost him a scholarship, Snavely invited Dad to his office, where he greeted Dad with an application to UNC. The coach's name was handwritten on the top.

"Walk this over to the admissions office," Coach Snavely said.

My father had never been able to afford a single ticket to a college football game—not even at Penn State, so close to Bellefonte. Now football *was* his ticket. He showed up in Chapel Hill two weeks later in a five-dollar suit with another five dollars in his pocket. Both lasted him four years.

We knew what football meant to Dad. Steve and I came to love football too.

So we never complained about the side trips to see stadiums. Besides, my father repaid our patience a million times over. If we had a hobby, Dad fed it, even if it meant going an extra mile ... or hundreds.

When my father was teaching and coaching football and track at West Forsyth High School in Clemmons, North Carolina, in the mid-1960s, he was awarded a scholarship for summer classes through the school system to be used at a college of his choice. Having been in Cheyenne, Wyoming, for military training after college and just before his marriage to Mom, he had long since wanted to show her the Great American West, and he chose to study at the University of Colorado-Boulder in the summer of 1966, with Steve and me in tow.

That summer, we enjoyed trips almost daily through the Rocky Mountains—along the front range on weekdays, farther west among the taller peaks on weekends, and throughout the state before all was said and done. By then, my brother was almost eighteen-months old, so traveling as a foursome was just becoming feasible.

Towing a pop-up camper, we bounced and skipped halfway across the continent until we landed in an apartment that we'd reserved in Boulder. We would later loop all the way to the California coast north to Seattle before heading back east.

Over fifty years later, I still have memories from every chapter of that trip. I remember the smell of our canvas car-top luggage carrier; I remember the last look at the house as we drove down the street and chanted:

"Bum-bum-bo, here we go!"

I remember the reflection of our car and camper in store windows as we rode slowly through dusty Kansas towns. I remember how the Rockies slowly rose up like a wall of thunderheads as we headed across the high prairies of eastern Colorado. I remember a rainbow near Colorado Springs that was so solid with color that I wanted to climb to the top of it and gleefully slip down as if on a playground slide.

There were the Great Salt Flats, the raw, cold, foggy Pacific Ocean shrouding the spires of San Francisco's Golden Gate Bridge, and the Seattle Space Needle. And I recall the green dinosaurs at every Sinclair Service Station west of the Mississippi River, most offering gas for nineteen cents a gallon then.

I *really* remember the Sinclair Stations. Like almost every five-year-old boy, I loved dinosaurs—I read about them, I drew them, and I dreamed of owning one. My bedroom was a testament to the Mesozoic era in crayons and modeling clay.

On that trip, however, I was too young to understand detours, diversions, and deadlines, so the fact that my parents devoted an entire day to bringing me to Dinosaur National Monument in Utah was underappreciated. If we had skipped it on the way to California, I would never have been the wiser.

Today, I hardly even remember the place, but more importantly, I remember *being* there, which is more important anyway—certainly more important than museum store-bought trinkets. The best souvenirs gather dust on a shelf; the best lessons are undying.

Dad would fuel my curiosity again and again over my youth through side trips to the Smithsonian to see a full-size brontosaurus skeleton or an afternoon ride to see local dinosaur tracks or fossil beds in New England.

Later, when it wasn't about *dinosaurs* anymore, I collected rocks and minerals. We stopped at every rock shop and gem mine and museum there was—all for the love of some amethyst crystal or a chunk of fool's gold.

Now I often ask myself how much I would pay in time or gas or effort in the midst of some trip to create a memory or even change a life. *What would Dad do?* Chances are that he would honor our interests and teach us to build from them, the way Coach Snavely had with Dad's love of football in 1948.

I've tried to pass it on—to feed my wife's and my own children's passions and reward their curiosity.

On a family trip to England during the height of my then twelve-year-old son Harrison's obsession with the Beatles, we rented a car and set off across the country to Liverpool for an afternoon. He looked over the Mersey River in driving rain. He stood next to the stage in the Cavern Club where mop-top musicians had played, and he stood next to a tombstone marked "Eleanor Rigby." It was a full day out of our trip devoted to driving, but it provided invaluable memories for my son . . . and for me.

On a trip to southern California, we devoted an afternoon for my daughter, then twenty-two, to shop on Rodeo Drive in Beverly Hills. Sure, we might have visited the La Brea Tar Pits for my precious dinosaurs' sake (old obsessions die hard) or spent more time on movie studio tours. But my wife and daughter got to see the hotel that was the setting for their favorite movie, *Pretty Woman*. They shopped at Tiffany's and bought the cheapest thing there, just for that Tiffany's box it came in.

Someday, I hope that my son and daughter will generously feed their own children's appetites for something wondrous or mysterious. Maybe, by then, they'll also understand how it's not about the fossils, bones, or rare stones. It's about the grand and mysterious detour, how it adds to the experience, and how it can bring out potential.

Today, dinosaur models and fluorite crystals are tucked side by side in a trunk in my basement. There's not much value to them, but they're good reminders, and I wouldn't trade the memories for the most precious gems.

I still look for green Sinclair dinosaurs when I'm in the West. And I still don't feel like I've visited an American city or college campus until I've seen the local football stadium.

5

Leaving Bellefonte

Pierogies, Red Roost, and the Great Abyss

> Whoever fights monsters should see to it that in the process he does not become a monster. And if you gaze long enough into an abyss, the abyss will gaze back into you.
>
> —*Friedrich Nietzsche*

Bellefonte was a dichotomy. There was ornate Bavarian architecture next to smoky dive bars with advertising in blacked-out windows for Schlitz and Yuengling beers in flickering neon. Then there were the mansions of the historic district that looked like they were plucked from a Victorian glass menagerie and dropped into the geographic middle of Pennsylvania.

I pulled into the town and drove up Molasses Hill to the bed-and-breakfast I'd reserved, a gingerbread, three-story house with heavy doors, narrow stairs leading every which way, and wide floorboards that moaned with every step. It was dripping with figurines and historical curiosities—a stereoscopic viewer, a brass spittoon, and musty 1950s *Life* magazines everywhere.

After dragging my luggage from the car amidst a rain squall in the gloaming, I quickly changed and made a getaway out of Bellefonte and a few miles northwest for dinner with my father's surviving family in Milesburg. There were nieces, nephews, half-brothers, and half-sisters who I'd never met and who my father barely knew himself.

Dad's sister, Laura, had passed away prior, but one son, Ron, and his wife, Joyce, were more than eager to host. Being of Polish descent, Joyce asked weeks prior if there was a Polish dish she could fix for my visit. Not wanting to show how unschooled I was in Polish culinary arts, I replied with the only Polish food I knew: "Um, pierogies? Is that a thing?"

Joyce replied with an eager "yes," and prepared about a thousand of them. When she admitted just prior to dinner that this was her first attempt at pierogies—basically, potato and cheese dumplings—I felt horrible that I'd asked. It's good that they were tasty, as I dutifully ate about thirty.

After dinner, we cracked open the photo albums and emptied manila envelopes of faded, black-and-white photos. We spoke and laughed about family history and the area's history; we did *not* speak of politics (I dipped my toe in those waters once or twice and found the temperatures chilly among at least one who was present). Still, I had a delightful time, finding the descendants of Dad's mother and her myriad suitors an altogether witty and resilient lot who were blunt and of one mind in the assessment of the family matriarch—a bleak assessment my father would have surely shared.

Born in 1928, nine months before the Wall Street crash heralded the Great Depression, my father spent his youth in and around Bellefonte and Red Roost, Pennsylvania, but his bags were packed from the day he was born.

Bellefonte was a small community known for the healing waters of its nearby freshwater springs, most of which fed into Spring Creek. It was a wide, churning waterway encircling the town before making an eager exit northward toward Milesburg.

If there was a poor section of Bellefonte, it was Red Roost, a one-time pocket of self-sufficient farmers and limestone miners on the other side of Molasses Hill from Bellefonte's Victorian river district. It was a five-minute walk over the hill from Bellefonte, but it felt like a million miles.

Everything looked down on Red Roost, from the hills that surrounded it to the Bellefonte locals, and from Red Roost, it was uphill in every direction. There was little that remained now: the Red Rooster Diner and a few machinery yards surrounded by sumac, razor wire, rust, and ruin. There wasn't even a signpost: even the town *name* left town.

If he had needed it, my father had had good reason to leave. He barely knew his parents. Before my father was walking, his father, Harold, had left the area to find work. In the early 1930s, with US unemployment as high as 25 percent, one went wherever the work was—in Harold's case, Buffalo.

Dad's mother, Margaret, was another story. "And there were plenty of stories," Dad would say.

According to some, she "entertained" male guests on a regular basis, ushering them into her home through the back door (whether this was a means of gainful employment is still conjecture). Harold once returned to Bellefonte unexpectedly and chased off one of his wife's suitors—or "clients"—with the parting gift of a black eye.

Dad and his two-year-older sister Laura would play out on the dirt road in front of the house. A story was told that my father was once found sitting naked in a cardboard box in the middle of the street. Sometimes abandonment has nothing to do with distance.

Hearing of this, Harold moved Dad and Laura out of their mother's house and into the nearby home of Harold's mother and father, who were strict Mennonites. They allowed Dad a cot alongside their *umpteen* other children and, eventually, their children's spouses. Everyone worked; everyone prayed; everyone ate, though not much.

Laura got married and moved out at an early age, leaving Dad with his grandparents and their family through the mid-1940s. But older friends and extended family members returning from World War II told tales of mystical kingdoms like France and Germany (and Virginia and New Jersey . . .), which captivated my father. After high school and only months after V-E Day, my father enlisted in the US Marine Corps and left town for basic training at Parris Island in South Carolina. Bellefonte was never "home" again.

The military provided my dad's first taste of life outside Pennsylvania, a taste of Carolina culture, and his first view of an ocean (or indoor plumbing). Following his military service, he hitchhiked from Bellefonte to Los Angeles, where he stayed until his money ran out—about ten days. After returning east and "Forrest Gump-ing" his way into college, he met my mother, Jackie, just a year behind him at UNC, and they married in 1954. I was born in 1960; my brother arrived in 1965. My father's life took many fortuitous and unpredictable turns, any one of which might be the subject of a book. But I consider here neither his constitution nor his fate nor his fortune—just his drive.

During college, the few dollars Dad could earn and save were spent primarily on bus tickets until he refurbished a car with his brother-in-law Joe during a brief summer visit back in Bellefonte. It was a 1947 Chevy, gray—as gray and lifeless as the sky, the grass, and the faces in the few surviving childhood photos. Once it was running, he kept that car for years. It was the last car he would own before the ones I remember riding in.

My earliest memory of riding with my parents was in our Volkswagen Beetle. When my mother wanted to keep the car for the day, she'd tuck me deep into the pocket of space behind the back seat and then drop my father off at his high school teaching job in Clemmons, NC. There I'd ride, bundled up in swaddling clothes like the baby Jesus, just in front of the engine and rear tire wells. As the car road over the final three-hundred-yard gravel road to a teachers' parking lot, the rocks thrown up against the tire wells sounded like artillery. I was three years old, and I thought my life was ending. That probably amounts to my oldest memory: fear of death in the back of a VW Beetle.

By the time my brother and I were old enough to be packed into a car for a trip of any length, my father had bought the Dodge Dart wagon, and we were off on a cross-country trip, introducing in 1966 a melody that I've been humming ever since. After we moved to Massachusetts in 1967, we made regular trips up and down the Atlantic states as my parents traveled to and from North Carolina and Mom's family. Every Sunday, we drove through the small towns and countryside of western New England.

Dad rarely lived far from an interstate highway. If you've found yourself imprisoned by your circumstances, you forever after leave the door ajar. One eye's always on the exit. At the heart of it, Dad lived for the next journey, and either as fate would have it or by design, a highway on-ramp was infrequently more than a stone's throw away.

I was never limited like my father was. I was never bound by geography or situation—Dad made sure of that—so I'm not sure where my own wanderlust comes from. But God help me, it's in me too. A couple days in one place, and I'm looking for a road out, if only for a few minutes or an hour or an afternoon—through the mists, down the road, or around a blind, forested curve.

The ride back to the bed-and-breakfast in Bellefonte that night was mired in a soupy mist. I got up the next morning to more rain.

Jesus, does the sun ever shine in central Pennsylvania?

After breakfast, I headed just a half-mile around the bend to Red Roost. Tucked somewhere in the sopping forests beyond dilapidated homes and up a precipitous hill from rusty construction yards was a limestone quarry. It had been abandoned for nearly a century, and ever since, water had seeped in, emerald-colored, dense, and fathomless. Presently, it only existed on Google Earth and in Dad's happier childhood stories—and God knows they were rare.

Whatever paths he and friends regularly beat from Red Roost up to the precipice of the quarry were gone. Ignoring warnings that the area was inhospitable and teeming with copperheads, I rushed in as fools do. I knew there were cliffs on my side of the quarry, but my hope was to follow the rim until I found the more gradual approach to the waters at the far end, roughly three hundred yards away. There, I'd cast upon the waters just a few ounces of ash I'd distilled from the "Comet can" into a plastic bag.

I was lost within the first hundred yards, but I soldiered on, wildly zigging here, zagging there, clumsily hopping up and down slippery, moss-covered boulders, and falling no less than a half-dozen times before turning back. I re-emerged from the area's practically impenetrable underbrush two hours later, having spun around in circles through thorny briars but never having seen the quarry where Dad once splashed and played.

While I'd hoped to spread some of my father's ashes in its green waters, all the foraging had afforded me no view of the abyss, and I swear I heard Dad's voice at one point:

"What in heaven's name are you doing?" it said. "If you're doing this for me, just *stop it*."

Be it imagined or otherwise, Dad's voice was calm, clear, and wise. It was the first time I felt I'd heard it in years without the filter of his dementia. I spread the ashes in tall grasses at the top of the slope. Defeated, wet, and disillusioned, I figured the rain would eventually wash the remains into the depths.

I spread a bit more of Dad's ashes in what was Red Roost—some in the angry, roaring waters of Spring Creek where my father used to swim (and in which one of his half-brothers had drowned) and a bit more where I supposed his grandparents' house might have been.

I didn't measure out how much was spread at each location, though it was modest. I had a general idea of places I wanted to engage in the ritual, but it was symbolic. It wasn't a recipe.

It didn't matter how *much* of Dad was left anywhere. It only mattered that he *was*.

I crammed myself back into my car, itchy and chilled, and I pulled from my pocket a damp photo of my father at age six or seven, looking forsaken and hopeless. I wanted to reach into the picture and take the hand of that boy with so much loss and sadness in his eyes and tell him how much brighter his life would someday be. I wanted to tell him how much brightness he would bring to others' lives—to *my* life.

I took another look around at that cramped little valley and the hills that hemmed it in like prison bars. There were no livable homes there anymore. There were no people—only ghosts and echoes.

It was easy to imagine it the way Dad might have seen it: confining and suffocating. I lay the photo on the dash, and I sobbed through the final strains of a playlist of songs I'd culled. Some of the songs were Dad's favorites; some were just emblematic of his journey. Others were just on the playlist because I *knew* they would make me cry. And God knows, I *needed* a good cry.

Jesus, I've only been in Red Roost a few hours, and I'm inconsolable.

Alas, whereas I'd been provided no gaze into the infinite abyss on this particular day, clearly, the abyss had gazed into me.

Leaving Red Roost, I headed back to the bed-and-breakfast to clean up, check out, and then walk to the Bellefonte historic district a bit. As a few rays of sunlight broke through the pallor and dappled the streets and a riverside grassy park, a sense of calm washed over me.

Maybe there was something to the healing waters of Bellefonte.

I'd survived torrential rains and floods of emotion, and I'd been left at peace. But like my father over seventy years before, I, too, was eager for the interstate. I plotted a course and made a quick exit onto I-80 East. As I hit the highway and turned up a playlist I'd called "Escape," the skies opened up wide and blue across central Pennsylvania, and I tearfully belted out songs filled with love and hope and power chords until my voice gave out around Wilkes-Barre.

Hell, I'm not even sure what the songs were. I just know if I heard them in thirty years, I'd probably lose it all over again.

6

Western Massachusetts

Sunday Drives, Beechnut Gum, and Fields of Play

> I know people who are so immersed in
> road maps that they never see the countryside they pass through, and others
> who, having traced a route, are held to it
> as though held by flanged wheels to rails.
> —*John Steinbeck*

The morning's rains were gone, as was my melancholy. Port Jervis, the Hudson River, and Connecticut were looming. I could feel my blood pressure dropping with every mile.

Taking a right turn onto US-84 eastbound and up the long climbs east of Scranton reminded me that this area of Pennsylvania offered one of the most beautiful drives on the Atlantic seaboard.

To be fair, I love the Rockies in the summertime, with their peaks still capped in white and their seasonal run-off roaring like thunder. Or in the fall when aspens set the mountainsides ablaze. Or the White Mountains of New Hampshire in autumn, when colors carpet the hillsides and frame the back roads and when maple leaves lay sunbathing on ancient stone walls.

On trips through the Delaware Water Gap, however, I've noticed scenery to rival any. Rolling hills shove trucks into slower lanes, where they pant and gasp for breath on longer climbs, so cars are treated to panoramas which stretch out over three states. Sugar maples begin to dominate the forests and lean in from the shoulders.

Moving eastward and crossing the Hudson River, colors seemed a bit brighter, the air seemed a bit cleaner, and the sunlight seemed a bit crisper. The sun painted only the treetops of higher hills, and time slipped by in the twilight.

I called ahead, picked up a pizza, and pulled into Ted's house in Simsbury, Connecticut, at around 9:00 p.m. I crammed into thirty minutes as much conversation as I could with my old friend and Dartmouth classmate Ted Fleming and his wife, Kathy, before retreating to a remote bedroom in their large, meandering home. I drew the shades on a day that felt like three days in one and set up my white noise machine, but it all sounded like the highway to me. On the edge of sleep, I bolted awake several times thinking I was still behind the wheel, before I finally succumbed.

Early the next morning, I cursed the daggers of light that slipped through the curtains. I smelled coffee and heard low hum of voices rooms away. It was 6:00 a.m., and everybody in the world was up but me.

A reunion with my closest high school friends in my old hometown of nearby Agawam, Massachusetts, was set for later that day, but I first had to drive the back route through Southwick into Agawam from western Connecticut. It wasn't long before landmarks—even the ones nearly obscured by strip malls and new housing developments—began to trigger memories of a million Sunday drives and adventures.

Growing up, we were made to travel. Our family was a foursome—a family built for front and back seats, two by two. Piling into the car was like changing into a perfectly-fitting pair of old jeans.

Our family road trips—those lasting days or weeks—generally were of two varieties: an extended visit with relatives or pure adventure (and often a bit of both). At least one leg of trips to and from Massachusetts and my mother's family in North Carolina was along I-95, the main corridor paralleling the American east coast and the older US Route 1.

The highway ran from Maine's border with New Brunswick south to southern Florida. It connected all the east coast metropolises, though we'd usually jump on around New Haven and dismount south of Richmond on our family trips to and from North Carolina.

We made that trip dozens of times. Before we'd even back out of the driveway in Massachusetts, we could guess where the worst traffic would be, which rest stops were safest and cleanest, and which exits had the most convenient drive-through

McDonald's (and this was before GPS or Google). We knew what to pack, what to leave behind, what sights were worth seeing, the ugliness that wasn't, and the landmarks worth waking up for in the wee hours of an overnight drive.

If we were also visiting my father's sister, Laura, in Bellefonte or her grown sons nearby, we would loop farther inland, taking I-84 West through the Delaware Water Gap to Scranton, I-81 South, and I-80 West right into Bellefonte. You could hear the roar of trucks on I-80 from Laura's house.

Those were our Christmas trips, spring break trips, and summer vacation trips, and we looked forward to each. But what I remember almost as well are shorter trips—the overnights to the New England coast, the weekends in the White Mountains of New Hampshire, or even the Sunday afternoon drives.

With the longer, multi-day trips heading south or throughout the farther reaches of New England, we might plot out only the quick escape route and then a road back. But with the shorter excursions, the routes were almost always in question. Often, the destination was simply the direction.

"Let's head west," Dad might say, "and maybe hit the Berkshires."

Maps were handy but getting lost was more fun—I think it was the goal sometimes. Sights, attractions, and oddities were always surprises, and the pace of both our drives and our conversations were leisurely and familiar.

Initially, these trips helped us escape the drudgery of apartment living in Springfield, Massachusetts, years before we moved to Agawam. It was a community we shared with elderly widows and retirees, young couples, and a number of sketchy individuals who would come and go with fluidity. We'd lived there while Dad was studying for his PhD in physical education at Springfield College, and the place was a means to an end: my parents couldn't stand it there.

They plotted a move up and out, teasing themselves with homeownership as they read real estate ads in bed late on Sunday mornings. Sunday afternoon drives were a reprieve from apartment living. They were necessary—sacrosanct even. We'd be out the door the second Mom finished making the day's post-church cups of Sanka and after the early round of NFL games were over.

In the front seat, my parents talked and laughed and conspired. To this day, I have no idea all that may have passed between them. In the back seat, my brother and I giggled, groaned, occasionally grew carsick, and bickered incessantly over legroom. When we reached an impasse, Dad would shoot a look across the front seat, and my mother would reach into her purse and pull out a pack of Peanut Butter Cheez Nabs, a Macintosh apple, or a stick of gum—Juicy Fruit if we were lucky, Beechnut if we weren't. In 1969, these items were "mental health foods," at least for my parents, who had put up with discord and griping from the back seat for just so long. But when Mom opened a pack of Beechnut gum inside our car and we chewed, the entire car was suddenly minty-fresh. To this day, I get carsick when I smell it.

On rainy day rides, we would eventually pull into some general store along the back roads of Berkshire towns—towns named for either a wealthy English family (Chesterfield or Williamsburg) or the local Indigenous Peoples (Quabbin or Nichewaug). Dad and Mom would tread the weathered floorboards and breathe in the thick, ancient scent of old pine and woodsmoke while my brother and I hunted for strings of rock candy or Dots or Charleston Chew candy bars. We never saw Mom or Dad buy candy for themselves, but every so often, I'd see Mom sneak a chunk of a Mr. Goodbar to Dad that she'd brought from home.

There were no video games or cellphones. On the road, my brother and I looked to see how many different states' license plates we could find in ten minutes. We gestured for truckers to sound their air horns. We played word games or tried to solve conundrums and riddles Dad would pose. When we grew bored of all of that, we invented something else. Or we'd just argue. The car windows were our monitors. Simple conversation was our social medium. And yet we still survived these horrifying dark ages.

On more hospitable days, Dad would mitigate backseat rancor with a stop at some park or simply an open field of grass. When you're eight, ten, or even twelve years old, everywhere is potentially a playground. There was little grass where we lived in our apartments, so a big open field would be Boston's Fenway Park or Green Bay's Lambeau Field, where we'd run and throw and jump and tackle and dive and roll on the ground until we could no longer.

Eventually, we'd stop at a Wendy's or a McDonald's to finish the ride. Between the sugar high, the resultant crash, the exercise, and the fast food, my brother and I would often sleep all the way back into our driveway, the itch and odor of fresh grass still strong with us.

As Dad terminated his studies at Springfield College and applied for teaching and coaching positions, some of the rides got longer. Trips for job interviews from Hershey, Pennsylvania, to Ithaca, New York, left me with dreamy memories of picnics and playgrounds across the northeast.

But wherever we rode and however groggy I was when we pulled back into our hometown, I could feel our neighborhood growing closer. Half-asleep, with eyes still closed, I counted the turns from the interstate to our door. Around the rotary, another half-minute of sleep. The ticking of turn signals, the sound of the road, the shape of the trees that loomed above us. And when that soft comfort would be torn from us, a harsh reality with all its blazing light and sharp edges was standing ready to descend again.

When Dad finally cut off the engine, the silence stung in our ears.

Home from a Sunday Drive

Autumn leaves were swaying silhouettes,
Beneath the quickly waning day,
Sunday eves were cast in violets,
Where pinks and reds and yellows played.

Mother yawned, Father drove the car,
Behind them, weary, I lay curled,
With grass-stained knees, my battle scars
Below their rearview-mirror world.

Longing, suckling this repast,
Of confident serenity,
Gently cradled soft and fast,
Within this brief infinity.

Postcards quickly passed us as we'd ride,
The towns, the faces, rolling hills,
Lapsing into almost-dreams, inside,
I'd never know a pace so still.

The tires' sweet strains: a lullaby,
One-note, sustaining boundless!
Sinking into light repose, I,
Would never hear a song as soundless.

And with each dormant free association,
Time and distance were consumed,

Until outside, above, realization,
Passing, high above they loomed:

The landmarks, through half-opened eyes,
Towering steeple, then a tree,
Hazy friends against the darkening skies,
Each familiarity.

Seconds on that veiled internal clock,
Counting down each turn we'd make,
I'd doze 'til each persistent gentle rock,
Softly nudges me awake.

And then the noise, enveloping and ringing,
Deafening, this silence, pure,
Reluctant birth, now bitter, cold, and stinging,
Home, and all that is unsure.

The next two days, using Ted and Kathy's house as a launching point, I made several trips through northern Connecticut and western Massachusetts to visit old friends, relive old glory, and look for old haunts. On the first day in Agawam, I enlisted the help of an old friend and classmate who was now a teacher at my old high school.

He gave me a heady tour of Agawam High School and then opened the gates to the old track where my father had coached. For the first time since leaving Pennsylvania, I spread a few of my father's ashes. I chose the finish line area where he'd explain the workouts to me and those teammates who would become my lifelong friends, many of whom I would see for dinner later that day. In this very spot, Dad would joke with us, tease us, and challenge us. Then he would assign our workout, but, more than that, he would explain why—what the benefits would be. As a high school track coach myself, I've always tried to do at least as much, instilling in each athlete not only fitness but an understanding and a love of running.

I then drove to the junior high school nearby to spread some ashes where Dad also taught and coached football for decades. The school was closed for the summer, so I couldn't visit the gym, but the football practice fields where outdoor gym classes were also held were right where Dad left them. The grasses were growing long with the summer season, and a pasture past the fields was already dense with corn, which stood like a wall against the turf. As I sprinkled ash into the air, soft late-afternoon breezes stirred across the far pasture, and I half expected to see Dad emerging from the cornfield like the ghostly characters in the film *Field of Dreams*.

"Hey, Ran—is this heaven?"

"No, Dad," I might reply. "It's Agawam. Wanna have a catch?"

I'd already regained a sense of my father from Pennsylvania that I'm not sure I'd ever truly understood. To sit in rainy, raw

Bellefonte and Red Roost was truly to see and envision him as a young boy of no consequence. On these playing fields, my father treated everyone—regardless of talent—as an athlete of equal worth and standing. Everyone mattered. Here I remembered Dad as I hadn't seen him in twenty years: robust, dynamic, funny, patient, insightful, crack-smart, respected, loved.

It was like visiting another old friend for the first time in years. It resurrected a notion of my father out from under the shroud of bedsheets and belligerence and nurses and dementia. Those horrid images were slipping out of focus, and my father was reappearing out of the mists.

As I arrived back at Ted's house to pack for the next phase of the trip, we shared updates on our families and local headlines. Once we'd caught up, the themes grew richer as we reminisced about Dad, my mother, my own family, and fittingly finished with a number of stories that had *not* changed through the years.

Like how Ted and I met at age eight. And how we both got into Dartmouth at the same time. Or how we formed an acoustic group with whom Ted, with his formally trained voice, sang Bob Dylan and Joe Cocker songs like opera. Or when we staged Ted's bachelor party as a hike of Mount Washington, the highest and most challenging climb in New England. Our kinship was that of brothers, and we sang out the stories like lyrics to an old, familiar song. I'd truly missed my friend, particularly so since Dad died. If I'd forgotten how much, I remembered now.

Since Ted would be driving us to our Dartmouth College reunion in his car the next day, I brought Dad's urn upstairs to my bedroom and placed it on the bedside table. I patted the old UNC Tar Heels baseball cap that sat atop the urn and smiled.

"There you go, Dad," I said, adding that I'd be taking a short trip with my friend and that I'd be back in a couple days . . . *"Now don't you go anywhere."*

My father, Maurice "Gus" Young, at age six, shown here outside his two-room schoolhouse in Bellefonte, Pennsylvania, in 1935, where he began an education that would end in a master's degree and doctoral studies.

Hitchhiking back from a short stay in Los Angeles, California, my father (far left) first rode with an ex-serviceman and his wife (second from left and center, respectively). En route, he was assigned the role of designated driver for a visit to this cantina in Juárez, Mexico, in January 1948. With neither a license nor driving experience, he drove the couple back to the United States later that night. Also shown are a young mariachi band musician (far right, rear) and a woman (far right, front) who made her designs on my father apparent throughout the evening.

On a visit to Bellefonte, Pennsylvania, from college at University of North Carolina at Chapel Hill around 1950, Dad (left) and his brother-in-law Joe Howard (right) rebuilt the engine on this Chevrolet. It would serve as my father's transportation for the next eight years.

Snow was piled high during winters of 1955–56 in Caribou, Maine, where my father and mother spent their salad days while stationed at Loring Air Force Base.

After graduate school in Chapel Hill, North Carolina, and three years teaching in Hornell, New York, my parents moved in this Volkswagen Beetle to Clemmons, North Carolina, where my father began a job teaching and coaching in 1961.

The trip to the West in 1966 was the first for our family foursome. My father (right) and I stopped for a picture on the road to Estes Park, Colorado, near the entrance to Rocky Mountain National Park.

The 1966 trip west eventually delivered us to the Pacific coast and San Francisco, California, where we enjoyed a breakfast in the foggy shadow of the Golden Gate Bridge. Shown, left to right, are Dad, Steve (eighteen months old), myself (five), and my mother.

The 1966 trip through Rocky Mountain National Park in Colorado made for this photo opportunity where my father (right) and I steered the waters of Poudre Lake east and west in accordance with the Continental Divide at Milner Pass.

The Milner Pass visit and photo op have been reprised several times. Here, my daughter, Alexa (left), and my son, Harrison (right), posed for a similar photo in 2006.

My wife, Kelly, snapped my picture at the same location in 2021, almost fifty-five years after the first visit.

Always the educator, "Coach Dad" still volunteered with several youth athletic teams after his retirement and his move back to North Carolina. He helped to introduce both his granddaughter, Alexa, and grandson, Harrison, to track and field, a sport both grandchildren would continue successfully through college.

Even when my father's coaching days were through, he and my mother would travel to see their grandchildren compete in high school and college meets throughout North Carolina. After cheering on Alexa and Harrison as they did at this invitational track meet in Greensboro, Dad and Mom would invariably take the long, scenic way home.

7

Dartmouth and Northern New England

Proper Tools, Cows, and "the Zombie"

> The best laid schemes o' mice an' men,
> Gang aft a-gley.
> —*Robert Burns*

I was looking forward to the two-hour journey to northern New England. I'd always thought that the Connecticut River Valley between Vermont and New Hampshire reflected what it might look like if God did away with people and greed and vitriol and started over with milk and honey. This day's drive would give us a taste.

After two very full days in western Connecticut with Ted and Kathy and catching up with my old friends in Massachusetts, Ted and I piled into his car and wound our way northward on pastoral Route 202 through Suffield, Westfield, and Southampton. Before hitting I-91 in Northampton, we rode under an array of ancient railroad trestles and past nineteenth-century town commons, quads, and gazebos.

Textile mills, "packies," and furniture stores in pre–World War I brick buildings cast old world shadows on modest downtowns.

Once on I-91, however, the remaining eighty miles to our Dartmouth College reunion in Hanover, New Hampshire, felt like it passed by in minutes.

As we rolled over Vermont's soft hills, we might have been the last people on earth, left alone with the pastures and, to our right, the Connecticut River that carved a path between them. There were few signs of life, save for cars and cows—there were far more cows than cars, in fact, which was probably true anywhere you traveled in the Green Mountain State.

"Five percent culture," I said, "and ninety-five percent agriculture."

Ted and I talked about everything under the sun, which only made periodic appearances, dancing on the grassy hilltops of southern Vermont. And Dad was ever-present in our minds and our conversation, as he'd been almost a father to Ted. The stories we recited had been told so many times that they had their own mythology. But there was also laughter amid the reverence. There was neither a pretense nor sadness about our discussion—we shared tales about his wit and wisdom easily, as if we could stop at a rest stop and call him to verify a bit of his history.

As Ted and I neared the exit for Hanover, New Hampshire, my thoughts landed on a particular adventure along the hilly highways through the Green and White Mountains involving several of my Dartmouth classmates.

A few days after sophomore fall finals, several friends and dormmates conspired to make a trip up I-89 to Sugarbush Ski Resort, just south of Burlington, Vermont. One group left in a sardine can of a car in the afternoon, but another load of us had to wait for a ride that evening in a car owned and driven by a terse and sardonic junior we had always called "the Zombie." He wasn't a person of many words (unless those many words were "fuck..." or "*fuck!*").

We college boys certainly lacked the foresight or industriousness of the generations before us, including Dad's. We didn't even look at the weather forecasts. At that age, we felt we were invulnerable to danger, or often with Dartmouth students, "Mummy and Daddy" would cushion the fall.

We didn't typically pay attention to the weather—we only responded to it. In fact, we heard only modest news of the Mount St. Helens eruption, the Reagan shooting, John Belushi's death . . . or of the world outside Hanover at all, really. Hell, we only had one television station—an NBC affiliate out of Claremont, New Hampshire, with so-so reception, and it ceased broadcasting promptly at midnight, halfway through *The Tonight Show* with Johnny Carson. Cable TV entered the picture around 1981, but only a couple fraternities got on board from the beginning. The real news was hard to come by, and we often ignored it anyway. We were interminably pampered and sheltered from the outside world and any distractions it might pose, so we had no idea that a major snowstorm was bearing down on us.

It started snowing as soon as we left Hanover. About a third of the way up I-89 to our destination and with three passengers in the Zombie's Volvo, we were traveling sixty miles per hour in blinding snow. Around Sharon, Vermont (famous for its meme-friendly sign: "Entering Sharon"), a vehicle from an on-ramp pulled onto the highway right in front of us and, for whatever reason, hit the brakes. We missed their car, but we spun about 180 degrees counterclockwise, leaving us still heading northbound, *backward*. But the Zombie overcompensated, and we spun around 360 degrees clockwise, leaving us in no better shape. Finally, he wrestled with the wheel such that we found ourselves pointed in the right direction again... still traveling *at fifty miles an hour.*

No one spoke for five minutes. No one wanted to jinx it or offer that we'd all died miles back and just hadn't realized it yet. There was some talk of it once we arrived at a condominium near Sugarbush, but it was discounted by those already there as frat-boy hyperbole. In fact, my own family to this day discounts the entire story. They tell me that we certainly never should have survived. Then again—and hear me out—maybe we *didn't*.

It was the Monday night John Lennon was shot in New York. We didn't hear about that tragedy until the next day because we weren't listening to the car radio, and we had had no way of listening to the news.

But we could sure as hell tell you the weather.

Borne of the Great Depression, American industriousness may have helped the Allies win World War II. Though not the stuff of history texts, it also helped my family survive many a winter storm.

The father of a friend of mine landed in the second wave at Normandy shortly after D-Day. With a stronghold on the beach at that point, the focus was town-to-town fighting across northern France. As if German resistance wasn't enough, simply making headway across soggy French farmlands had become difficult. Rain, mud, and thick hedgerows hindered the tank and vehicle deployment and disillusioned foot soldiers.

Hitler had bet heavily that the Allies would break down and stall without equipment repairs and replacements, and that would be that. He hadn't counted on the Allies' determination and, more importantly, the ability to look at everyday items and see new uses. As it happened, US soldiers went to French locals and borrowed blades from snowplows, welding them to the fronts of tanks, which then sliced easily through dense thickets. And that was that.

This ability to rethink and repurpose may seem alien to later generations raised on a disposable goods economy and overnight obsolescence. Members of "America's Greatest Generation" would tell you that little was discarded during their youth. Very few items were useless, even when that use wasn't what the item was intended for.

Dad had also grown up during the Depression. He believed that nothing was to be tossed out until it was either rust or dust.

When we moved Mom and Dad into assisted living, Steve and I had to clear out the house before putting it on the market. This was hard enough given the distractions, as each and every item seemed to evoke a Christmas memory here or a road trip recollection there. Cleaning out a backyard work shed Dad had built, however, it became apparent Dad had never met a screw, a nut, or a bolt he didn't love. He must have picked up and saved every nail or washer he ever found. There were millions.

"You know," Dad would say, "just in case."

It seemed like Dad could take a pencil eraser and a bottle cap and *MacGyver* an airport terminal out of thin air. A lot of folks from my father's generation possessed the same skills, but where Dad really stood out was in frigid weather. He knew how to drive and keep a car running in the cold—he knew the hacks and workarounds.

In addition to the resolve and frugality that the Depression instilled in Dad, he left boot camp at Parris Island a week early for an assignment as an airplane mechanic at Cherry Point

Air Force Base in Morehead City, NC, where he learned his way around engines and motors.

Between college and graduate school, Dad enlisted as a second lieutenant (thanks to ROTC) at Loring Air Force Base's Caribou Air Station near the town of Limestone, Maine. Stocked to the brim with B-52s, it was a large Strategic Air Command base. It was the closest point in the continental United States to Europe by air, making it a perfect headquarters for the 45th Air Division, supporting the 42nd Bomb Wing.

My father banged around in every nook and cranny of the contiguous United States. He white-knuckled his way across the border into Mexico, and he visited Canada several times. But for all the miles my father logged, Loring was the closest he ever got to Europe. In all likelihood, Dad never visited Europe simply because he couldn't *drive* there. In fact, if there had been a bridge built across the Atlantic Ocean, Dad would have been off to Europe in a heartbeat.

Life in Caribou and at Loring AFB helped my parents adjust to temperatures of minus 40°—that's −40° Fahrenheit *and* −40° Celsius: deadly cold by either measure. Dad said he once spat in those conditions and it froze before it hit the ground. More importantly, though, he knew what *wouldn't* freeze.

This was demonstrated one frigid evening decades later, in February 1979, during my senior year in high school. I was to run at the Indoor State Championship track meet in eastern Massachusetts, and we drove to the meet as a family.

The competition ran until mid-evening on a Saturday, but snow had begun falling around 5:00 p.m. The temperature had dropped into the teens, it was dark, and the roads were a mess. Our car started, but we weren't going anywhere. The tires just spun with the whir of a dentist's drill.

Worse, we couldn't see. The defrost was no match for the ice accumulating on the windows, and the wiper fluid reservoir had frozen solid. Dad got out, scanned the parking lot, lifted the back door of our station wagon, and began to scheme.

He calmly went to a corner of the lot, returned with two large cinderblocks, and put them above the car's rear tire wells for ballast. He next walked to a grocery store around the corner and returned with only kitty litter and red wine. Dad tossed a few handfuls of litter around each of our four tires for traction. Then he poured a cheeky little merlot into the wiper fluid reservoir, knowing the high alcohol level might prevent freezing, at least for a while.

Lastly, Dad opened a small jackknife from his key ring and carefully stabbed it into the valves on all four tires, allowing just a bit of air out of each. This allowed the tires to soften a bit and provide more surface contact with the road, thus more traction.

We were on the highway in minutes, though Dad kept to the posted speed limit. The smell of cheap wine followed us all the way home, which might have been hard to explain had we been pulled by police.

Examples of our father's industry were everywhere. If the world didn't fit, he made adjustments.

When we lived in apartments, he decided that Ted and I deserved a basketball hoop to shoot at, but there wasn't one nearby. So he fastened a standard hoop to a rough plywood backboard and attached large question-mark-shaped hooks on the back, so we could hang the contraption on a fence or railing above any stretch of asphalt. The only difference between a parking lot and a play space for Dad was brainstorming and a few screws.

In our house in Agawam, old steam heat radiators would clank and hiss incessantly during winters, and the air was insufferably dry. Dad didn't buy a humidifier, though. He figured he could provide the same effect by placing pans of water atop each radiator. Rooms, once saunas, were now steam baths.

Others weren't as impressed with my father's jury-rigging, however. Through our late adolescence, my brother and I found ourselves apologizing to dates for various Rube Goldberg machinations that kept our cars on the road. A bent coat hanger kept a front window vent from continually flying open. Coca-Cola was kept in the car to strip rust off lug nuts when changing tires.

But when the windshield wipers began to fail on a green GMC Ambassador my brother and I typically drove in high school, Dad ran a rope around both wipers, strung it across the front seat, and tied it off in a large loop. This allowed both Steve and me to really make impressions on first dates on rainy evenings by keeping one hand on the wheel and the rope in the other hand, which we tugged back and forth to move the wipers.

Steve and I both resorted to this tactic on numerous first dates. We had far fewer second ones. Today, my car has a length of rope in it. Maybe it's not for the windshield wipers, but who knows? There are coke bottles under the front seat. There are a thousand screws and washers, batteries, and flashlights throughout the vehicle.

"You know," I explain to my own kids, "just in case."

After all, things do "*Gang aft a-gley.*"

Ted and I left Vermont behind, crossed the Connecticut River, and pulled into Hanover, New Hampshire, at around 3:00 p.m. Picking up the key to a shared suite in the same dormitory where we'd spent our entire four years of college, we found several old dormmates congregating in a room near ours. Across from me in the room sat the Zombie, though most now referred to him as Dr. Zombrowski, MD. We all talked and talked and laughed aloud at incredulous lies and tall tales until, during one precipitous silence, the Zombie sidled up next to me and spoke.

"So, that drive up I-89 in the fucking blizzard," he began. "My family doesn't fucking believe the story. That *did* fucking happen, right?"

8

I-91 South to Connecticut...

Ghosts Stories, Camping, and the Sacred Silence

> I think ninety-nine times and find nothing. I stop thinking, swim in silence, and the truth comes to me.
> —*Albert Einstein*

When our 1965 Dodge Dart died, it was hard to move on. We were already prejudiced against the new 1972 Dodge Coronet Custom station wagon my father purchased. We also had every reason to believe that, right off the assembly line, the car was haunted.

That summer, during a visit to our grandmother Luna in Chapel Hill, North Carolina—"Granny Lu," we called her—we packed her into the backseat between Steve and me and set off for a five-day trip-within-a-trip to the Carolina coast.

We stayed in a house just yards from the beach with my mother's first cousin Mabel, her husband, Walker, and their children, who were much younger than Steve and me. Moreover, these three boys were absolute savages who Walker spanked publicly and with regularity throughout our stay, altering their behavior very little.

The house stayed hot twenty-four hours a day and smelled of coconut suntan lotion, low tide, and Chef Boyardee SpaghettiOs. Over the course of our days there, I suffered from sunburn, I was stung by a jellyfish, and I was nearly carried out to sea by a riptide. My mom's brother, Jim, drove Granny Lu's Plymouth K-car down and met us there about three days into our stay as well, which tipped the scales toward sanity at least. But by day four, my father—typically diplomatic to a fault—spoke up at a dinner on the subject of Walker's parenting-by-paddling.

"You know," he directed at no one really, though all were present, "I've never respected folks who feel it's necessary to continuously spank their kids in public. I mean, doesn't it seem like a weak and gratuitous display of power? It's obviously just for show."

It was time to leave.

On our final day, we packed up our mustard-yellow Dodge and Granny Lu's K-car and made a sightseeing trip farther south for the South Carolina coast and Calabash-style seafood. Afterward, stuffed and sleepy, we started back toward Chapel Hill with Mom driving her mother in the K-car and Jim riding shotgun next to Dad in our new station wagon, while Steve and I occupied the backseat.

There were no major highways serving the southern coast of North Carolina at that time, and it was as dark as pitch outside. Steve and I had slept for about an hour when Dad pulled off to get gas and use the bathroom at some A-frame gas station in Warsaw, North Carolina, conveniently located at the intersection of nothing and nothing. That should have been a sign.

"Anybody need to go?" Dad asked, hearing no reply. "Well, okay..."

Dad filled the tank with gas and then headed off for restrooms while Jim remained in the car with us and, seeing Steve and me stirring a bit, offered up a ghost story. I've little memory of the tale now. But we knew it would be a cool story because Jim was cool: he played jazz—he knew John Coltrane and played alongside Chick Corea, Dizzy Gillespie, and Stan Getz—and he would season his stories with colorful language that we wouldn't hear from Dad, like "damn." (Earlier in the evening, Jim had even said, "Shit." Dad winced, but Steve and I giggled in spite of ourselves.)

By the time Dad returned to the driver's seat and started the car, Jim's story had reached a climax, and he drummed the approaching footsteps of the story's axe murderer or witch or ghost by pounding his flat hand on the dashboard.

"Thump . . . Thump . . . went the footsteps," Jim said. "Thump..."

On about the fourth "thump," however, a piercing buzzer sounded from under the dash somewhere, abrasive and as loud as a factory whistle. We all jumped.

"SHIT!" Jim shouted.

"Okay, *now* I have to go to the bathroom," I said.

"Me too," said Steve.

In the months we'd been driving it, the Coronet had never made this sound. Dad thought it might have been an engine alarm or something—maybe low oil pressure.

"Jim," Dad said, "you broke my new car?"

But as the adults investigated, Steve and I realized the truth: the car was simply haunted. Each time Jim and Dad got out of the car to investigate under the hood, the buzz disappeared. They would re-enter the car and take their seats, and there it would be again. Clearly, there were ghosts about.

We rode all the way back to Chapel Hill with that air raid siren in our ears, only to discover later that alarms went off in newer cars when front seatbelts weren't fastened. Dad later tried to disable the feature to no avail and simply had to buckle up.

It may not have been a ghost, but it still ranks as one of the most memorable ghost stories Steve and I ever heard, if for reasons that were completely unintended.

I'd been reminded over the course of the reunion that Dartmouth folk were a different lot. In talking to some Ivy League alumni, you'd hear about their alma mater within thirty seconds. It would generally take you hours of solid conversation to learn of a Dartmouth pedigree if it wasn't printed in faded letters on their beer-stained t-shirt.

I'd forgotten how unpretentious these folks were. It was a nice reminder that I belonged to a society where the average intelligence was superseded only by humility. Dartmouth was distinguished, as author Bill Bryson described it, "by an air of privileged endeavor and the presence of five thousand students, not one of whom could be trusted to cross a road in safety."

Many alumni were closet success stories; others still couldn't tie their own shoes. Over the course of the four-day reunion weekend, however, I had lunch with the legal advisor to the California cannabis lobby, I chugged a beer under a reunion tent with a federal investigator who helped to bring "Whitey" Bulger to justice, and I went halfsies on a pizza with the founder of Shutterfly. On the other hand, I witnessed one very distinguished and rich alumna who, over three drunken days in the reunion tent, seemed to have melted into a lawn chair that burped and spat insults into the air.

By that Sunday, it was time to head out. I had a long, long way to go on this day. I would spend one last morning in Hanover, head south to reunite with my car—and Dad—at Ted's house by early afternoon, and drive all the way to Baltimore by that evening.

I'd ridden part of the way north a week earlier on the more pastoral route, but today would be spent traversing I-95 and the interstate highways that my family had navigated on so many trips between New England and North Carolina.

By 10:00 a.m., Ted and I had said our goodbyes and made one last costly stop at the jam-packed Dartmouth Co-Op for overpriced ballcaps and koozies. With one more lap around the campus commons, we headed back across the Connecticut River and connected with I-91 southbound in Vermont.

I'd planned out so many playlists and conversations for our assault on Hanover and the recapture of youthful exuberance that I hadn't thought about the departure. Now that it was over, I already missed these people. I missed having the event to look forward to. There was little remaining to do on my trip but return home. All that was left were final goodbyes, and the air seemed thinner now, reflective, and less charged with anticipation. I'd gorged myself on conversations for four days and enjoyed every minute of it. Still, I felt sated, and the conversation was now sparse between Ted and me. He wasn't talking much either. As we rose and fell around the wide turns of Vermont, even music seemed like an intruder—a blasphemy.

These were my final hours and minutes with my best friend, who was unofficially a member of the Young family. At least Dad had always treated him that way, and Ted had thought of Dad as a father. Having been all but abandoned by his own father, Ted had more in common with Dad than I'd credited.

Crossing the border into Massachusetts, we would soon be descending on Amherst, Agawam, and Springfield, and finally, Simsbury, Connecticut, to pick up my car at Ted's. Along with the final chapters of this adventure would come a few final revelations, a few final handfuls of ashes to be spread, a few final tears to be shed, and a final goodbye to my father.

There were a million words hanging there right in front of us, but none needed to be said. We rode comfortably and quietly for a good spell, and it seemed fitting. We weren't interested in shortening the trip with idle discourse, and the sacred silence sounded like a hymn.

The Yogi Berra Museum and Learning Center in Little Falls, New Jersey, openly speculates that the former New York Yankee is quoted more often than William Shakespeare. Dad didn't typically quote the Bard, but he quoted (and misquoted) Berra with regularity.

The fact that I love word games, puns, and conundrums is owing to Dad's love of language (at least spoken language, as he was never really a reader). He often amused himself with Yogi Berra-isms, like, "No one goes there nowadays—it's too crowded." Or variations, like, "I love it when it's completely quiet, because only then you can hear everything."

He loved suppositions that were both completely nonsensical and utterly true.

There is so much to hear in silences, and we treat ourselves to so little of it. Silence may be golden, but we wrap ourselves up in noise like a blanket. The TV blares when we do housework; the car radio blasts because the *next* song may be better than the last. Grocery stores play soundtracks to distract us from how much we're tossing in the cart. Gyms play music that motivates us to "get pumped," and service stations now blast commercials and "life hacks" while we pump our gas. If we're ever sitting alone in silence, we check social media because we don't want to miss a text or a post or be the last to hear about *anything*.

But, for all the sound, we don't listen very well, nor do we look at each other for long or even sit side by side and stare out at the world in amazement.

We are addicted to sound, be it happy, funny, or irritating. Some have lamented that we need the cacophony of media and smartphones to distract us from real emotions—that we're avoiding the abyss of sadness or self-doubt that creeps into rare silences like a thief in the night. (This abyss doesn't intimidate me, though. I've been to Red Roost, Pennsylvania.)

I think the modern "noise dealers" are already aware of all of this. The radio and television peddlers and pundits know that if we ever dared to shut down the feed, we might discover mindfulness and sobriety in the sound of our own thoughts— we might understand that we don't need their drug. They don't want us to discover this, however, so the noise plays on. After all, in live broadcasting, "dead air" for longer than a few seconds is unforgivable, as if listeners might begin to channel surf after a millisecond of silence.

It's this conspiracy of noise and information that steals from us unapologetically, as does time. This makes it so easy to see why silence—real silence and not mere quiet—is a rare blessing.

Shut it all down—the radio, the phone, the conversation—and we're still besieged with messaging. At precisely the posted speed limit, the surface of historic Route 66 east of Albuquerque, New Mexico, is grooved to play "America the Beautiful" on the passenger-side tires. Well enough for some, I think, but if traffic is moving slowly, I suspect this wonderful hymn would sound like a funeral dirge. If you want to inspire me, take me to a stretch of highway that plays Beethoven's Ninth or Pink Floyd's "Comfortably Numb." Or even a stretch of highway that makes no sound at all, for it's only in that silence that we might hear our thoughts or the Composer's voice.

Aldous Huxley said, "After silence, that which comes nearest to expressing the inexpressible is music." Yet even classical composers insist that rest notes are as necessary as the melodious ones—silences sing too. There is such a symphony at work on the roads and highways, but we rarely hear it because we fear it. That's why I often turn off the radio or podcasts or tapes or CDs or streaming and let the road play its own melody. There's so much to hear.

There's a rhythm to the road, for example. Only decades ago, the United States was teeming with concrete highways. Scarring of the surface for traction provided a steady hum. Control joints scored into highway slabs to prevent cracking of the concrete provided the percussion: *"Ga-dunk ... Ga-dunk ... "*

With these "beats" spaced evenly along a stretch of scored highway, you are composing music as you move.

But the road itself is only a fraction of the orchestration, which also includes growling gears, rumbling engines, brassy horns, and piccolo-pitched squeals of truck brakes. Rain hissing beneath the tires sounds like bacon frying on a skillet. An open window on a summer drive provides the roar of ocean waves at a full gale.

Inside the car, we were in the orchestra pit. In the Dodge Dart, triangle-shaped vents next to the front seat windows would be cracked so Mom could often hold her Benson and Hedges 101 cigarettes to the draft and smoke would be drawn out. With a tap of her finger, sparks flew past our rear windows like shooting stars. All the while, the window whistled a pitch as insistent as a kettle brought to boil.

I do think the rare silences bring us closer to a truth. They encourage us to *think* without being fed *what* to think. They invite us to enjoy a richer intimacy with the countryside, road, sky, or fellow travelers that you can't see and hear sitting in front of the flat screen at home.

Many families sought this kind of communion with the elements by going camping or hiking. Some families built campfires, told ghost stories, ate s'mores, and saw each other's eyes sparkle with firelight as the dark world outside of that sacred circle was held at bay. Later, everyone lay in their tents as only muffled conversations, muted laughter, and the sputter of embers in the dying fire remained.

Not us. Travel *was* camping out for us.

If we were not staying in a hotel, Dad just drove straight through to our destination to save money. Mom navigated, reading maps by the light of the radio dial or the orange flare at the tip of her cigarette. Our car was our campsite, our cabin, our tent, and our retreat, with the dashboard light for a fire, snacks, ghost stories, and the mysteries that lurked out in the darkness. We deliberated the nature of the universe, watched eyes sparkle with the faint glow from the front seat, and fought the unrelenting tug of sleep.

After a while, Steve and I would retreat to our pallet in the back and scratch primitive cave etchings into the cold frost on the windows on winter trips. We'd draw pictures of rockets and dinosaurs and stick figures of our grandmother's dogs and laugh until our stomachs ached. When we bit the frost out from under our fingernails, the ice tasted of the nicotine in Mom's cigarettes, stinging our lips and the tips of our tongues.

On long road trips through sleep-filled, featureless nights, cradled in the gentle rock and soft lullaby of a steady pace down the highway, I remember the sudden shocking hush when the engine stopped at a highway rest stop when Dad needed a break and a cup of strong coffee or Mom needed a look at the map.

In the whispers that entered our hazy half-sleep were the reminders that there were benevolent spirits only feet away, their faces painted in greenish hues by the dashboard light like the shadowy figures of a Toulouse-Lautrec painting.

The tap of my father's wedding ring against the steering wheel as he pulled back onto the highway and merged back into the night was the tapping of the maestro's baton. The symphony resumed. *"And the rest was silence."*

Shakespeare said that; Yogi didn't.

9

Connecticut to New York City

Rotaries, the Front Seat,
and a Thousand Cigarettes

> The wheel is come full circle.
> —*William Shakespeare*

I've known people who could solve a Rubik's Cube in thirty seconds but couldn't figure out how to enter a traffic circle. Grown adults. With driver's licenses. And *everything*.

   Just south of Northampton, Massachusetts, Ted ducked off I-91 and took back roads through western Massachusetts to West Springfield and a sporting goods store so that I could pick up some Boston Red Sox items for my family that I couldn't simply find at home. We happened upon a rotary entering my childhood hometown of Agawam from the north. If you were driving along the Connecticut River or crossing over it, the rotary was your only entrance into Agawam. You had to go around it at least once, though some drivers would circle the thing several times as they tried to figure out the right exit.

The rotary wasn't more than four hundred yards from my childhood home. I'd been on it thousands of times, but it had been years. I used to collect bottles tossed into its center and turn them in at the local convenience store for the deposit. I made $2.00 that way one day. I drove on it the day I earned my driver's license; I drove on it the day I left Agawam.

That rotary had become a family joke—Dad called it a meat grinder. Drivers flew right past yield signs and barreled onto the roundabout like they owned it. A sizable number of vehicles never made it off the bloody thing in one piece, victims of New England drivers' sense of self-entitlement. Inside the rotary was an elephants' graveyard full of fenders and bumpers stacked up like rusted bones: the tombstones of mishaps and tragedies.

That's singularly American, I think. We grab for points, win the race, beat all comers, and keep score of *every. Damned. Thing.* In my experience, rotaries work well in England and Ireland probably because the polite drivers there don't attack their roundabouts with photon torpedoes blasting.

Once upon this rotary, there were five exit choices. One would send me down River Road toward my old house; two more tangents led to Agawam's downtown. A fourth pointed across the Connecticut River toward I-91. The last exit spun drivers off toward the Massachusetts Turnpike (the "Mass Pike") and Boston or the Berkshires. A thousand adventurous plans were solidified by simply choosing when to cede to centrifugal force.

Every great trip in my youth began and ended with a calculated leap from that playground carousel. It was a watershed—ultimately, a place for choices: *Home or away? What to keep; what to abandon?*

Not until Granny Lu died in September, 1986, did Steve and I ascend to our places in the front seat.

I was out of college and living near New Hampshire's coastline. Steve was also at Dartmouth, just beginning his senior fall semester in Hanover, New Hampshire. It was mid-afternoon when I got the phone call telling me that Granny Lu had passed. I drove to my parents' house in Agawam, Massachusetts, and arrived later that afternoon; Steve was already there. Dad and Mom were already packed for a flight from Bradley Field International Airport west of Hartford, Connecticut, to Raleigh–Durham International Airport, North Carolina. They left just after we got home.

But while they flew, we would drive. It would be a rite of passage. Steve and I would head south overnight in my 1984 Chevy Chevette, following the same route our family trips had always taken. But this time it would be without my parents; this time, *we* were in the front seat.

The occasion notwithstanding, I was looking forward to the adventure and pulling a highway all-nighter with my brother.

By 6:00 p.m., we were spinning off the rotary toward Springfield's South End Bridge, bound for I-91 and then I-95 South.

In our car was our luggage, liters of Mountain Dew soda, a map, two cartons of cigarettes, and a *very* experienced football.

A mid-evening arrival at the Cross Bronx Expressway and the twilight beyond the George Washington Bridge would send us cascading through New Jersey, chain-smoking and singing to Billy Joel and Mr. Mister with the windows down. This made for an odd mix: the sour sting of nicotine and chemical stench wafting out of the local landfills and tidal marshes. It hung in the air, a pink-lemonade haze as thick as lobster bisque beneath the towering halogen lights. Inside the car, the dash and seats were tacky with it. You could feel it on your skin and taste it on your tongue.

Once every mile or so, the land leveled out to our left and the Manhattan skyline rose proudly out of the mists, first the World Trade Center's Twin Towers, then the Chrysler and Empire State Buildings in Midtown. To our right, the last radial spokes of a zodiacal twilight shone over Newark Airport, the Meadowlands, and the travel plazas that slid by every five minutes or so.

The cause was solemn, but the tone was almost playful. Maybe in grieving one death we were reveling in our own sense of immortality. We smoked like we were out to set a record.

Between the exits, on-ramps, and intertwined highways, it was easy to feel smaller than the road, swallowed up by the moment or miles. There was no response but to push on through the night, marking our progress one toll booth at a time. With the glow of the boroughs now sinking in the rear-view mirror, New York was the last dying ember in a fading fire, and nervousness crept over us. For all the chaos of that noisy stretch of road, we knew that hours of unbroken darkness lay ahead.

We were on our own now, but the path was paved. Even half-asleep in the near light, we honked in the Baltimore Tunnel, stopped into rest stops for old coffee, traced our fingers along lines on maps, and watched the sun rise over the Virginia–North Carolina border.

To be honest, I don't remember much about the stay in North Carolina. I don't remember the relatives or the church or the eulogy, and I was still a bit road weary when we turned around and started the return trip north a couple days later. Steve and I rested for a night in Agawam and then headed our separate ways the next day, spinning off that same Agawam rotary in different directions toward our different worlds.

I saw Steve off, taking an extra lap to watch him disappear. He jabbed a middle finger out of his window and shot off toward I-91 North and Dartmouth. A lap later, I peeled off for the Mass Pike and the New Hampshire seacoast.

As for the trip itself, we'd now taken our place behind the wheel and made it over hundreds of miles of highways and thousands of ghostly towns and numbered exits ramps that disappeared into the night.

There was a mountain of meaning to that original trip. Ultimately, we'd said goodbye to my grandmother, but it was also a goodbye to the weightless, carefree, unencumbered view of the world from a seat in the back row. Steve and I would never truly call Agawam "home" again, and I knew it would never play the same character in our lives. Neither would the rear seat of our parents' car.

For these reasons and others, I found it surprisingly hard to say goodbye to Steve and to pack the adventure away. Until that trip, he'd always been my *little* brother. Forever after, he would simply be my brother.

It *did*, however, help to inform a common, enduring lexicon. These jokes, comments under the breath, revelations, or mere acknowledgments, when reprised, commemorate shared experiences and provide a sense of permanence, like a holiday tradition or a ritualized family joke at family gatherings.

"Did you fart?" Steve had asked as we passed just south of Weehawken, New Jersey.

"No," I said. "That's Newark."

And around ninety minutes later . . .

"Delaware is in dire need of a new state motto," Steve said as we crossed the Delaware River toward Wilmington. "Maybe something like, 'Please disperse. . . . There's nothing to see here.'"

Ted and I rode lazily along the last few back roads to his house in Connecticut and a reunion with my Subaru Outback... and with Dad. My trip was in its last leg now, and this fitting goodbye to my father at seventy miles per hour was almost complete.

I spent little time at Ted's. I was eager to rip off the Band-Aid and get on with it. It would be one last grueling blast down I-95—the same route Steve and I had traveled thirty-two years prior. Finally, there were hugs, tears, and waves in the rearview and a reunion with Dad, who sat beside me again in the front seat.

"Missed you," I said, patting Dad's UNC cap atop his urn and fastening both of our seatbelts.

If all went as expected—allowing for the usual gridlock on New York City's Cross Bronx Expressway—I'd be across the George Washington Bridge by early evening, south of New Jersey by sunset, and honking in the Baltimore Tunnel by mid-evening before arriving at my hotel in Glen Burnie, Maryland, just south of Baltimore.

About twenty minutes after the goodbyes at Ted and Kathy's, I was already on I-91 South. Out and back was now simply *back*. It was the homestretch, and my head was swirling with thoughts of Dartmouth, my friends, Dad, Ted, and my first trip south with Steve. As New York City loomed, I cued up Mr. Mister's "Broken Wings" on my playlist and uttered the melancholy howl signifying any grand return:

"Bum-bum-bum, here we come..."

A circle is a round straight line with a hole in the middle.

—*Mark Twain*

10

I-95 South to Maryland

Dad's Duffel, the Maryland House, and Unicorns

> Sport is a universal language, building more bridges between people than anything else I can think of.
> —*Olympic Runner Sebastian Coe*

By the time I reached New York City, I'd only been on the road a few hours, and I was already ninety minutes behind schedule.

"You are still on the fastest route to your destination," Google Maps said.

On this day—and almost every day—the Cross Bronx Expressway was a hot, sticky parking lot. It had retaining walls for shoulders, about an eight-inch margin between cars, guardrails, and a river of refuse tossed from neighboring tenement high-rises. Any less than ninety minutes from the New York–Connecticut border to New Jersey's Vince Lombardi Rest Area past the George Washington Bridge was light speed.

Running late was par for the course. I'd made a habit of taking on *A Bridge Too Far* on a regular basis, always planning too many events and destinations to pack neatly into one day. Oddly, I missed Kelly's constant reminders that our kids needed to eat dinner prior to 2:00 a.m. and that the decade-old beef jerky and trail mix under the front seat would not constitute a meal.

I would love to blame Dad's influence for this, but it's entirely on me, owing to the need to please everyone all the time, including myself. You know, so I can be popular. So people will like me. So I win.

Thus, many of my own family's salient memories on trips were chasing light, confirming reservations, or settling for late-night fast-food dinners in nearly empty restaurants a tick before closing time with the smell of bleach in the air. I can't count the number of times someone with a mop and bucket had to unlock the front door to a restaurant to let us out.

Even as I crossed the George Washington Bridge and lit upon I-95 in New Jersey, I knew I'd be eating late tonight, hopefully near my destination. Even so, I'd have to make up some time, so I flew through New Jersey. Exits were blurs. I wouldn't even stop to toss change in the toll booths which came along every minute. I would simply glide past for a fade-away jump shot.

I couldn't even afford a bathroom break, but no worries. Who needs rest stops when you have on board a hospital-grade HealthyKin male portable plastic urinal (with a handy angled design and easy-grip contoured handle)? It was my first time using it during the trip, but there were plenty of items in the car that were packed in a panic, envisioning those occasions which might call specifically for them.

Binoculars ... WD-40 ... Duct tape ... A football. *Always a football.*

There was an additional passenger in my father's car on many of our afternoon drives and all our longer trips: a tattered, old duffel bag full of physical education. Like a magic hat, it was a prop for Dad's act, whereby he would make needed things appear on cue out of thin air.

If Steve or I needed to stretch our legs or were bickering in the backseat, Dad simply withdrew a sporting goods item or two from the bottomless bag. *Poof:* a catcher's mitt ... *Bam:* a square-toed football place-kicker's shoe ... *Abracadabra:* a five iron and a basketball.

"Let's play," he'd say—one of the most important things any child can hear, boys or girls, young or not-so-young.

We'd find a playground or an open space, park the car, and dig into that duffel like it was Santa's pack. Out would come baseball gloves, ice skates, or tennis racquets. What also came out of that duffel was a basic syntax of almost any physical activity imaginable.

These were the souvenirs from that shared magical time in all our lives when, as the poet John Tobias wrote, "unicorns were still possible, and the purpose of knees was to be skinned." There was nothing up Dad's sleeve except the belief that learning a few humble skills in any sport was like speaking a second (or third or fourth) language. We weren't fluent in every tongue, but we spoke almost every sport.

In his book *Silent Night: The Story of the World War I Christmas Truce*, author Stanley Weintraub wrote of the cease-fire occurring during the early winter of 1914 on the muddy battlefields of Belgium. Spontaneously, British and French soldiers left their trenches that day and offered the German soldiers handshakes, food and candy from care packages, and the challenge of a friendly soccer game.

A real soccer ball was supplied by a Scot with the 133rd Saxon Regiment, and a regulation match ensued with caps laid out for goals. The Germans beat the Brits 3–2.

Fighting resumed quickly, and the Great War stretched on through another three winters. Attempts to organize similar truces failed, and millions more died. Still, for a few minutes, among men of disparate duties and beliefs, it felt a little less like war and a little more like Christmas.

If a pick-up soccer game more than a century ago might deliver a sliver of peace among sworn enemies, imagine what the essence of play might do between strangers in a park or a parking lot, where play can make for strange bedfellows.

During the same 1986 trip to Granny Lu's funeral, Steve and I found ourselves in that darkness that lay from central New Jersey to Delaware with just more nothingness until the Maryland House Travel Plaza.

The Maryland House was an I-95 rest stop sitting in the wide median between the north and southbound lanes, about thirty-one miles north of Baltimore. It was originally a simple two-story brick facility with questionably appropriate murals of the area's Colonial-era and Revolutionary War history to entertain visitors on their route to the second-floor bathrooms. A ground-level extension offered a buffet-style restaurant with burgers, fries, and snacks during regular hours but merely vending machines for late visitors.

It was I-95's own Casablanca, rife with foreign peoples halfway to exotic destinations like Tampa or Hoboken, all yelling at their children in strange languages at the top of their lungs.

Both Steve and I had foggy memories of the times my parents had woken us up deep in the night and walked us past the murals and up the stairs to the bathroom like zombies.

At such hours, there was always the smell of cigarettes and diesel fumes just outside and the smell of cleaner inside. But it also offered my parents the opportunity to stretch, take a breath, and unclench their teeth after braving either New York City traffic to the north or Washington, DC, beltline traffic just to the south.

If they visited from the northbound lanes, there would be nothing but pitch black for hours thereafter, and my brother and I would quickly tumble back into sleep again. If we were southbound, we knew it would only be a half-hour until the Baltimore tunnel, so we'd try to stay awake, but we never could. Instead, my mother would reach back and jostle us; we'd rise to our elbows, peak out the windows at the bright blur of passing tunnel walls, and plead with my father to "Honk, Dad! Honk the horn!"

(We insisted that he honk the car horn deep inside any tunnel, and he always obliged, maybe because we all liked the echo or maybe because the tunnel would collapse if he didn't.)

Maybe we'd wake up briefly an hour later to see the Washington Monument like an apparition out in the distance, but memories of anything between Maryland House and central North Carolina were generally hazy.

On our own trip in September, 1986, however, Steve and I saw signs for the Maryland House at around 3:00 a.m., and we pulled into the parking lot, accidentally taking the fork at the entrance road marked "Trucks." Tired, haggard, and buzzing a bit from both the nicotine and the miles, we stumbled out into the night and tip-toed around trucks like they were sleeping giants.

Going to the bathroom felt like revisiting a dream from childhood only to realize, *Wow, that* was *real?* Returning to the car, however, we decided we'd made sufficiently good time to earn a quick recreation break in the well-lit parking lot, so Steve grabbed the old football from the back seat.

We'd been tossing the ball around for less than a minute when truck drivers began to emerge sleepily from their cabins and called for us to toss them the ball. We didn't know these people, and we probably wouldn't give them so much as a nod in passing inside the Maryland House. But in the parking lot, we engaged them in conversation—not in words, but in the simple exercise in trust that is a game of catch.

It's a grammar learned from the earliest age. Often, before a child even speaks the words "Mama" or "Dada," they will roll a ball across the carpet or toss a spoon on the floor, just to see if it returns. Pick up the spoon and give it back to a child, and they'll throw it right back down on the floor again. It's frustrating; it feels like a meaningless exercise, but it's a lesson in motor skills. More importantly, it's a lesson in trust.

"If I give this away; you give it *back*." It's that simple.

Sure, Steve and I were technically in the wrong parking area, and these strangers were hardened truckers halfway through the night of the long haul, some of them twice our age. But for about twenty minutes in the Maryland House Travel Plaza parking lot, my brother and I and around a dozen burly drivers were a pack of kids in an elementary schoolyard.

Each driver gestured for the ball, saw it tossed high into the black night, grabbed it out of the air thick with diesel fumes, and danced in an asphalt end-zone as truck horns blasted.

And in that almost-perfect time and place, where the purpose of balls was to be thrown and caught and returned, and where suspicion and cynicism gave way to trust and joy and nostalgia and childlike wonder, unicorns were possible once again.

Reflections on a Gift of Watermelon Pickle

(Received from a Friend Called Felicity)
—John Tobias

During that summer
When unicorns were still possible;
When the purpose of knees
Was to be skinned;
When shiny horse chestnuts
  (Hollowed out
  Fitted with straws
  Crammed with tobacco
  Stolen from butts
  In family ashtrays)
Were puffed in green lizard silence
While straddling thick branches
Far above and away
From the softening effects
Of civilization;

During that summer—
Which may never have been at all;
But which has become more real
Than the one that was—
Watermelons ruled.

Thick imperial slices
Melting frigidly on sun-parched tongues

Dribbling from chins;
Leaving the best part,
The black bullet seeds,
To be spit out in rapid fire
Against the wall
Against the wind
Against each other;

And when the ammunition was spent,
There was always another bite:
It was a summer of limitless bites,
Of hungers quickly felt
And quickly forgotten
With the next careless gorging.

The bites are fewer now.
Each one is savored lingeringly,
Swallowed reluctantly.

But in a jar put up by Felicity,
The summer which maybe never was
Has been captured and preserved.
And when we unscrew the lid
And slice off a piece
And let it linger on our tongue:
Unicorns become possible again.

Just south of Trenton, New Jersey, I-95 splits without warning into a half-dozen I-95s. One minute, you're on I-95 proper; the next moment, you're on I-295 south, wondering if you missed an exit. In that vicinity, a very unsympathetic tollbooth attendant named "V. Ruffo" told me that the $17.60 I owed for the previous four miles' travel was not payable by debit card, promissory note, or hard labor. He promised me that I would be hearing from the New Jersey Highway Commission in the near future.

(The attendant was as good as his promise. An invoice featuring a photo of my license plate arrived in the mail a week later.)

Without having so much as changed lanes, I found myself on I-95 again south of Wilmington, Delaware. I compartmentalized my debt to New Jersey and focused instead on points south. Neither my bladder nor I were going to make it to the Maryland House Travel Plaza near Abingdon. Thank God I could simply pull out my hospital-grade HealthyKin male portable plastic urinal (with a handy angled design and easy-grip contoured handle) from under my seat as I crossed the Susquehanna River and arrived in Havre de Grace, Maryland. All that water only added to the urgency.

Use of the HealthyKin urinal (etc., etc.) should have been easy. It allowed me to concentrate on the road in front of me, and I would submit that at least a half of what was intended for the receptacle *did* actually end up in there. But the other half ended up just about everywhere else. If the window had been open wider, some would have gone into the Susquehanna. I think the handy angled design is where things went wrong. It was still another fifteen minutes to the Maryland House and a walk of shame.

As I arrived in the parking lot and headed inside, toting along a change of clothes, however, I was shocked to see absolutely nothing of the gloriously shabby old facility I remembered so lovingly. There were beautifully modern restaurants arranged in a food court and clean bathrooms.

I hate this.

There was nothing of the cheesy smorgasbord eatery I'd known, little of the parking lot where my brother and I had tossed a football, and no signs of the semi-racist murals I'd seen with my parents on late-night bathroom trips. Thomas Wolfe said, "You can't go home again." Apparently, you can't go back to Maryland either.

About a half-hour south of the Maryland House, I was honking in a tunnel beneath the Baltimore harbor and ready for the labyrinth of turns and exits that would land me at a Hampton Inn in Glen Burnie by midnight. By the time I checked in, the only local restaurant still serving food was a Denny's about two miles away.

The service was cold; the food was colder. To be fair, I wasn't at my best either, so who was I to judge? The restaurant smelled like French fries and bleach, and I probably still smelled of the highway and urea. I owed a letter to the quality control specialists at HealthyKin, and V. Ruffo had assured me that I owed money to New Jersey, which is not anything anyone wants to hear.

This day had made for a long *week*. I slept hard that night, dreaming of traffic and exits and tolls and my family and my own bed, now just a day away. I was nervous about my last leg of travel. I wondered what wisdom I might finally glean from my journey with Dad, I pondered on where I might spread the last of his ashes, and I feared the loneliness that loomed beyond that ultimate "goodbye."

11

Southbound on I-85 . . .

Dinosaurs, Dementia, and Delays

> Take a detour.
> Discover small towns and friendly faces
> that don't grow along the highway.
> —*Khang Kijarro Nguyen*

The heavy hotel curtains were drawn tightly shut. Very little light bled through, and the entire room clung greedily to darkness. On this day, so did I.

I was just as sullen about ending the trip as I had been giddy about embarking upon it nine days prior. When the alarm on my cellphone sounded, I hit "snooze" three times.

Finally, I just lay staring heavy-lidded at the silhouette of my father's urn on the bedside table and, beside it, the Comet can dispenser. There were at least seven hours of travel ahead, but that wasn't half as intimidating as my final obligation: spreading the very last ashes from the Comet can. I hadn't thought hard about the *hows* or *wheres*. I simply feared the finality.

Where would I look for Dad *after* this day? Where would he be if not in the urn and the remaining ashes? After this final undertaking, the task would be done. The can would be empty, and I sensed that I would be as well.

Shouldn't there be something more? Shouldn't there be more noise about it all?

For all the formality, I felt as if the spreading of my father's remains amounted to the splash of a single drop of rain into the sea. Wherever Dad was going, I felt he should arrive not with a tear or a trickle but a fanfare—a proud, roaring pronouncement. The world should shout out full-throated at the heavens above:

"Stand back, you angels, you ghosts, you martyrs and charlatans! Widen your gates and move aside, for a great soul is approaching. Make way, for it is a grand and restless spirit that enters into your midst."

Still, the only way through this day's solemn finality would be the way home. There would be an inherent sense of accomplishment in completing the appointed rounds of a road trip done properly. It was the signature at the bottom of a painting. I checked out of the hotel in Glen Burnie at 9:00 a.m., visited a Starbucks next door, filled up with gas, and thought out the course in my head.

By getting on the road early, I might even allow myself a quick dance through a couple Smithsonian museums on the Mall in Washington, DC, which opened at 10:00 a.m. I wouldn't have long—it would just be a couple tour stops: the Apollo Lunar Module, the Spirit of St. Louis, the Hope Diamond... *dinosaurs.*

Dad understood the melancholy that descends on the final day of any trip, and he would typically spring one last adventure on the family as we made our way home. When Dad carved out a visit to Washington, DC, into the last leg of a north–south trip in 1968, I'd already seen Sinclair Stations and Utah's Dinosaur National Monument. I was ready to be underwhelmed by the dinosaur exhibit at the Smithsonian.

But to this day, I remember it well. There had been a menacing T.rex skull at the exhibit entrance, a Triceratops skeleton, artists' depictions of Jurassic battles, and a half-ton Brontosaurus femur with a sign that invited kids to touch it.

After twenty minutes of circling the Mall for a parking space on this visit, I made it into the National Air and Space Museum, which had closed off about a third of the exhibition area for no apparent reason. Maybe they were running short on "space"?

Across the quadrangle, I entered Natural History Museum and moved from the main rotunda toward what *should* have been the dinosaur exhibit. Instead, there was fur. Some idiotic curator had decided to push the dinosaur exhibit back into the museum's nether regions. Those entering that same wing found themselves mired in mammals.

After *Jurassic Park* in 1992, maybe a stack of gray bones was uninspiring. Or perhaps, given a resurgence of nationalism at the time, throwing mammals out front made a statement given a rise of smug science-skepticism and a cult of creationism. Either way, for the second time in history, dinosaurs were clearly facing demotion in the scheme of things. It didn't take a comet this time—just a curator who got his cues from Yelp.

Survival of the fittest.

I returned to the car and checked my Google Maps app for traffic from Washington, DC, to North Carolina. A friendly male voice on my phone directed me southward on Route 310 instead of the direct I-95 South toward Richmond:

"Numerous accidents are causing significant delays on I-95. You are on the fastest route. Please get your ass into the left lane for a series of inexplicable U-turns."

"Shit," I spat. "Seriously?"

"Yes," I thought I heard the voice say. *"I never lie."*

"But what if the accident scenes clear up soon?" I pleaded. "What if traffic clears?"

"There are like eleven accidents. And they won't clear up. I'm seeing to that."

"But—" I began.

"Don't be stubborn. Get off the main highway for once. Seek a new route. Travel a different way. For God's sake, get lost once in a while."

"I'd prefer to get home today," I said. "Life's an out-and-back, and I need to get back."

"True enough. Life's an out-and-back . . . but sometimes the miles are crooked."

Suddenly, the voice I was hearing—either from my cellphone or in my head—sounded less like an app and a lot more like Dad. As I arrived at Route 310 South through

Maryland, I turned off the app, but not before it offered one final direction:

"*Sometimes the best road to take will leave you lost—lost in the right direction.*"

There are a few places in the world where time noticeably stands still. During a visit several years prior to England, my son, Harrison, and I visited Winston Churchill's bunker beneath the Treasury Building in the Whitehall area of London. Here, the small, gray rooms where plans to save the world were laid out now played host to Eastern Europeans and Americans in Hawaiian shirts who had already been to Buckingham Palace and Abbey Road.

All maps in the facility showed Allied troop locations in Europe as of the war's end. A calendar on one wall still showed the date as August 16, 1945, the day after the surrender of Japan, forever marking the last day the room was used strategically. In the same room where the first World War II cabinet was held, clocks reflect in perpetuity the start of the meeting: 4:59 p.m. on October 15, 1940. Clock hands stood eerily still.

Such was Route 310 South.

For the first time in nine days, I was a stranger on a strange road, forsaking smooth asphalt for worn, scarred concrete. I was on the alternate route, one I hadn't mapped out, leading through towns and countryside locked in time.

There were strip malls and fast-food chains and Jiffy Lubes in small towns, to be sure. But between them were old churches and homes pressed in against the road's sandy shoulders. Crossroads bore old family names, and private driveways led right out into traffic. Stacked on cinderblocks, rusted fins on old Chevys rose just above the weeds and stalked the tall grasses around trailers and bungalows like sharks. Mud puddles filled with spring showers still dotted the gravel driveways to live bait shops and flea markets.

At the same time, gas was cheap, lights were green, and the traffic was light. The scent wafting from fields of wildflowers was verdant, thick, and sweet. Banners waved proudly on little league backstops behind empty diamonds. American flags decorated porches where local gentry sipped iced sweet tea with lemon and mint leaves and waved or tipped a John Deere ballcap from their porch swings or rocking chairs.

This wasn't like Buena Vista on my first day of travel—that town just lingered behind others by decades. No, along this route, time simply stood still. Towns here appeared as if they had stopped evolving the very minute that I-95 was completed, reflecting the more practical option—the fastest route.

Again, I was looking through a glass pane at a museum diorama. I-95, like many modern highways, had struck like a comet, and only the prehistoric bones of these old towns were left to tell the tale of another era, both rustic and glorious.

Survival of the fittest.

It's odd how we can live in the presence of a monster and choose not to admit it. Perhaps it grows so slowly from day to day that it somehow makes it easier to live in its shadow than stare it in the face.

As Dad's and Mom's mental decline became more evident in the early 2010s, I took over more and more duties and helped where I could. The early changes could easily have been attributable to age alone and were almost laughable. Eventually, the laughter subsided.

Technology became a challenge. Dad would call about once a week, checking on how to watch a VHS tape on his Blu-ray Disc player or asking what all the colored wires were for. Mom would call daily with concerns about strange emails in her inbox or whether pop-up ads had killed her computer, which Dad had simply unplugged. In many cases, I wasn't sure if Mom and Dad had lost the ability to do things for themselves or if they'd never acquired them to begin with.

Astonishingly, I didn't blink an eye when I was notified by a local bank manager that my parents had tried to withdraw $2,000 "for groceries." I wasn't even alarmed when a neighbor smelled smoke and checked in on my parents to find that they had gone out for a ride while a frozen pizza cooked in the oven—still in the box. This nearly set the kitchen on fire.

Still, banking, shopping, entertainment, and cooking mattered little to them. It was *travel* that was their sustenance. If they couldn't pay bills, prepare meals, send emails, or record a single movie, they could still reheat old coffee saved in carafes in their refrigerator, jump into their car, and head off to parts unknown. The problem was that the "unknown" regions were growing more common. Roads and towns that were familiar just weeks prior were suddenly strange and unrecognizable to them.

When we eventually moved them out of their house into an assisted living center, Steve and I found dozens of carafes of coffee in the refrigerator, some dating back months or even years—coffee that would never be drunk on rides that would never be taken.

However, the first genuine shock for me was hearing that my dad had gone to buy gas but pumped diesel fuel into his Honda. He realized the mistake and was alert enough to have the car towed to a local repair shop, but the oversight would cost him a thousand dollars. This was nothing compared with the embarrassment Dad felt. After that, whenever I'd pop by for a visit, I'd simply borrow their car and fill up the tank. This, I would learn, was like handing loaded guns to children.

Eventually, Dad relinquished many of the driving duties to Mom. I wasn't worried when my mother drove into the in-laws' mailbox. I wasn't bothered when my mother drove for an appointment at a nearby doctor and called me from twenty miles past the office down an interstate highway. Dad was with her but was no help.

"What do you see?" I asked her, trying to discern her exact location.

"Well," she said easily, "there's this big boney fish."

There was an extended silence.

"Mom, you're at a Bonefish Seafood Grill?" I asked incredulously. "That's probably not where your doctor is."

"Well, that's what *I* thought too."

I stayed on the phone with Mom for almost a half-hour, talking her home, step-by-step, turn-by-turn, until they were back in their own driveway. There was no doctor's appointment. There never had been.

I am not seeking absolution. The fact that Mom or Dad might have been a danger to themselves or others on the roads never entered my mind. I was simply not ready to take the next step and rob them of a freedom most-precious: the ability to turn a key, hit the gas, and see the world. Steve and I looked into visiting nurse agencies; we investigated "Meals on Wheels." But while these options made sense, they would not fulfill my parents' need to escape the four walls around them and ride.

When things became alarmingly apparent, my brother and I looked at the situation more closely. We made the hard decision to move Mom and Dad into the memory care ward of a local assisted living center. (I often wonder if this was actually an easier choice than taking their car keys away.) To help with the costs, we sold their car and, a year later, the house.

Life happens quickly when you're not paying attention, and it happens at *blinding* speeds when you are. When we cleaned out their car, we found a receipt in the glove compartment from a convenience store in Virginia, nearly eighty miles away. On the back, in penmanship we didn't recognize, were directions back to Chapel Hill. Apparently, driving haphazardly from town to town hadn't been sufficient. Mom and Dad were now getting lost across state borders.

We moved them into assisted living that was only ten miles to the north and convenient to both Steve and me in Chapel Hill. After sixty-three years of marriage, Dad and Mom shared a room and awoke every morning to the remotely familiar smile of a perfect stranger in the other bed. Steve and I would visit them regularly, and I made doubly sure to free them every Sunday from those halls, the ubiquitous paintings of flowers and pastures and puppies, and that smell of age and confusion and decay.

I would help them both into the backseat, stop by a fast-food drive-up window for coffee, then perhaps drive south to visit the UNC campus where they'd first met, which seemed to pique their interests, even if they weren't sure why. We'd even drive past the very church where they were married in 1954. The university and town were changing quickly, however, as universities and towns do, and cognitive impairment notwithstanding, Mom and Dad might have had a tough time recognizing the place.

I'm sometimes curious whether the aged lose contact with the world or if the world simply grows strange and intimidating around them.

I never did take them past their old house, however, as the new owners traveled a lot for work and afforded neither an interest in any previous owners nor mowing more than once a summer. Bricks crumbled on the front porch, nails rusted, and back patio deck boards grew warped and misshapen.

I wondered how they would ever know that the set of Tonka trucks Steve and I got one Christmas was hidden in a backyard sandbox Dad had built, now buried beneath monkey grass and running ivy. Or that an old four iron lay beneath the kudzu toward the back of the yard. Or if they cared that the hand-built, wooden birdhouses that fed a thousand cardinals and finches and bluebirds now lay rotting beneath the back deck, home only to dust and spiders.

Even if we *had* driven by the house, Mom and Dad would not have remembered these things that lay rusting or growing mildewed in the shaded crevasses and attic corners. Only Steve and I remembered these things now. *Just us.*

So we avoided the house. Instead, we'd typically roll across the rounded hills and pastures of the local countryside for the sheer beauty. Dad would occasionally utter a comment as we passed a structure that sparked a memory:

"Oooh, that's a *go-back*," he'd say.

"What is?"

"That place," he'd state confidently. "I went there when I was in the military."

"That silo?" I'd ask. "You mean the *silo*?"

"Oooh, yeah."

Or Mom would see a modern ice cream stand by the roadside—

"Oh, my mother Luna loved that house."

Time is a thief—a truly vile, unprejudicial, unrelenting, unsympathetic bastard. But then there's dementia. Dementia not only robs us of what we are, but it also steals from us everything we ever *were*. Travel, I now believe, is either the cure or at least the best medicine to dull the ache.

Hot coffee became too dangerous to handle for my parents without help. Over only a couple of years, Dad grew quieter; Mom became less and less comfortable away from the assisted living center.

"Do you know how to get us back?" Mom would ask nervously, wringing her hands and fiddling with the dome light and every door lock and window button she could find, even the ones I would disable.

"Sure, Mom. I know the way."

"I think I'd feel better if we got back," she'd say, resolved. (Often, she'd start with this before we'd left the parking lot of the senior center.)

Eventually, conversation became almost impossible. Dad would start to put a thought into words, stumble on the idea, and then back off. Initially, I'd end up finishing sentences for both Dad and Mom. Later, I'd start their sentences as well. Eventually, there was just the engine, the wind, and the road.

But even though they were out of practice conversationally, I knew that somewhere in their souls, they were more comfortable on the road than anywhere else in the world. I knew that the rides fed them. I'd watch them in the rearview mirror as they gazed out of open windows, smiling softly as waves of grains rolled by.

I wondered if they saw Steve or me once like I saw them now. I wondered if Dad had once glanced in his rearview at the similar sight of Steve and me, fifty years before, swaying with the soft curves, sunk into safe recesses, drunk, dreaming, and drowsy on the miles as we floated down back roads and highways.

There, low in that back seat, confident in our captains, we are all children once again. We are oblivious to past or future or age or time, quietly gazing out at the earth and sky and stars in a constant state of awe until a billion breezes whirl and whisper their secrets or roar their resolve, and a trillion twilights drape the skies in lavender.

Out and back. And so it goes . . . until, trip by trip, town by town, turn by turn, we are delivered home safely, the lights dim, the silence descends, and "the long trick is over."

Everything south of the Potomac felt like it led to the twisted conglomeration of byways that coursed through Richmond, and it wasn't long before I began to see signs for I-95 again. From that junction, I estimated a time of arrival, and I called Kelly at home to let her know I was safely on my way.

However, with rush hour traffic between Richmond and Petersburg, Virginia, the going was slow—even slower than Route 310. It would still be three hours, which gave me time to deliberate further on where I would empty the last of Dad's ashes from the Comet can.

Richmond itself is altogether unremarkable from I-95. To be fair, the highway doesn't get its hands dirty. It soars over the city at a safe height, never touching the ground, never socializing, barely mingling with the local streets and alleys. From that vantage, Richmond barely enters the picture. It's a blur, a passing glimpse out of the side window at a bustling southern city fettered by a legacy of slavery and tobacco. It suckles at the breast of the James River, a waterway so dirty it once caught fire in the mid-1990s.

Around twenty-five minutes farther south, Petersburg was Richmond-lite. It reflected all of the histories of Richmond but without the large colleges or progressive ethics of the New South. It was where I would leave I-95 for I-85, however. From there, it was simply a long driveway to my doorstep, as I-85 would bring me to within a few miles of home.

By day, I-85 from Petersburg southwest to the North Carolina border passed *by* towns and not through them: Dinwiddie, Baskerville Mill, and Alberta warranted no mention. Road signs were rare; exits were scarce. Trees were plentiful, however. Dense groves that leaned in from the shoulder, hiding farms and towns, also ran thick through the median, hiding northbound lanes entirely. It was a narrow, slot canyon trail of a highway, carved cleanly through poplars, longleaf pines, and old oaks as if by a sharpened knife.

Without streetlights, I-85 was notoriously dark after sunset. Just to the west was Virginia's Staunton River State Park, which was officially recognized as an International Dark Sky site. Since most north–south traffic opted for I-95 to the east, one could drive I-85 for twenty miles without seeing a single set of headlights.

This evening, as I sped through these primeval woods around dinnertime, the driving was easy. But as I mulled over the remaining business I would address, a thought suddenly occurred to me. If it was to be the last morsel of silent reflection, what better place to release the final wisps of Dad's ashes than on the stretch of road that likely greeted Dad when he first arrived in North Carolina?

In 1948, he was coming home too. He just didn't know that at the time. He'd never truly known "home" before.

This is where he was, I thought. Maybe *this* is what he saw.

With that, I reached for the dispenser can of ashes, carefully twisted the lid loose, took a deep breath, and released most of my father's remaining ashes out of the window and into the winds and the wilds near the North Carolina border. I immediately felt . . . nothing.

Nothing: no closure, no clearer picture, no revelation, no epiphany.

What the hell was wrong with me?

I'd spent years attending to a diminished version of Dad: a vague, confused, struggling ghost of a once-invincible force of nature, given to unpredictable outbursts and anger. I'd gone so diligently about the business of caring for my father that I'd never said goodbye to Dad. Dementia and age had robbed me of that.

Maybe I was just not doing it right.

As I looked into the can and saw only a few grains of dust remaining, I tried to remember where they'd gone.

The images from the trip came to mind, and I smiled as each washed over me. The ashes had trickled into a gorge where my father had escaped his circumstances and swam as a child. They'd fallen into a rushing stream that had pointed the way out of town and out of a dark adolescence. They'd been laid upon fields of play where my father had spent his career confidently sharing his love for sports and recreation. And they'd now been scattered on the road that connected him to North Carolina ... and me.

I could see all those places now, and I could see my father there. He did not look diminished. He was not struggling. He was not in pain or lashing out at strangers. He was ... Dad. Where my father had come to be possessed by someone unrecognizable in his final years, there had now resurfaced this image of curiosity, vitality, and strength.

There he was, Goddamnit. *There he was.*

Tearing up, I reached for the Comet can once more and felt the lightness of it. Without hesitation, I thrust the open end out of my window and shook from it every last curl of smoke and ash.

It was now an empty vessel, without meaning. There was nothing of my dad left there. But there really never had been. It had *always* been empty, really. My father had truly *never* been in it. Like the stranger that wore my father's face for so many years, there was no more of Dad in *that* empty vessel than there had been in this can.

I looked into the rearview mirror and watched my dad's dust swirl in the drafts and eddies in my wake. Then my gaze moved to my own reflection in the driver's seat, where, just for an instant, I thought I saw Dad's face where mine should have been.

Author David Mitchell wrote, "When you travel far enough, you meet yourself." Maybe there was more of my father in that reflection than anywhere I'd looked for him. Here, through me, he was in the front seat again; here, he was at the wheel. The road belonged to him again, just as he now belonged to the road. I'd never felt closer to the journey, closer to what moved my father, or closer to him, and I cried for thirty miles.

As the first signs for Durham and Chapel Hill began to appear on mileage markers, I opened all the windows and felt the wind softly buffet my face and shoulders. The air smelled of the South—rich and sweet with the fragrance of pine that gave hints of juniper and gin. The sun sank into the rich red earth of family farmlands, and fireflies just began to light their flames beneath the deep, dark, wooded canopy.

In every sense, it already felt like home. I've found that nothing reinforces that sensation in me like returning from a long and eventful journey. By the time I sailed south along the long, narrow bridge which seemed to float atop Falls Lake just north of Durham, North Carolina, I felt like the air itself might carry me home from there. I was completing this round trip and certainly richer for the miles and the adventures.

I dried my eyes and wondered at what had been revealed. After all, if I could rediscover a living memory of Dad in the man now behind the wheel, was I providing as much to my own family as he had his? Had my own children come to see me as I saw my father?

Would my children someday share warm memories of their own dad setting a course for adventure, adding chapters to the mythology, uttering the incantations, invoking a bit of magic, and passing along a bit of wonder?

If I could believe that I have been the tour guide for my children that Dad had been for me, now *there* would be a journey, a life well spent, and another family brought under the road's spell.

Another lap.

Out-and-back.

> Allons! the road is before us!
> It is safe—I have tried it—my own feet have tried
>   it well—be not detain'd!
>
> Let the paper remain on the desk unwritten, and
>   the book on the shelf unopen'd!
> Let the tools remain in the workshop! let the
>   money remain unearn'd!
> Let the school stand! mind not the cry of
>   the teacher!
> Let the preacher preach in his pulpit! let the
>   lawyer plead in the court, and the judge
>   expound the law.
>
> Camerado, I give you my hand!
> I give you my love more precious than money,

I give you myself before preaching or law;
Will you give me yourself? will you come travel
    with me?
Shall we stick by each other as long as we live?

—Walt Whitman
Song of the Open Road, 15

Epilogue

> Our life is an apprenticeship to the truth that around every circle another can be drawn; that there is no end in nature, but every end is a beginning, but every end is a beginning; that there is always another dawn risen on midnoon, and under every deep a lower deep opens.
> —*Ralph Waldo Emerson*

Dante Alighieri (1265-1321) describes in his narrative poem *Divine Comedy* the ninth level of Hell not as an inferno but as a dark, frigid place in which Satan himself is frozen into the lake Cocytus.

After returning from my trip north, I spent days on a couch in my basement, weeding through boxes of newspaper clippings, letters, military paperwork, and photos. Since the thermostat was upstairs where it was warmer, the basement was air-conditioned to a fault, and I spent a good deal of time shivering. There was little outside light down there. There were no clocks, but unlike those last towns I'd passed through in Virginia, it wasn't locked into a time—it was timeless. Old photos from our family life mingled with ancient black and white photos from Dad and Mom's wedding. Despite the trip and all its revelations, it was a hellish place to sit and reduce a man's life to dusty paper and faded pictures.

Against one wall was an antique pie cabinet. My father's urn now sat on top. Inside of the cabinet were several items suited to a humble shrine: an old stopwatch, Dad's wedding ring, a Bible given to him by a cousin when he left Bellefonte for the military, and a few old football programs from UNC featuring his name and photo.

As I sorted which would be stored in boxes and which would be relegated to the "Hall of Fame" cabinet, I came across a box of letters Dad wrote to my mother over the months before they married in 1954.

Having graduated from UNC and participated in ROTC, Dad was a first lieutenant stationed for three months of training in Cheyenne, Wyoming. Mom had graduated in 1953 and was working at the Durham (North Carolina) Center for the Blind. The letters were yellowed and brittle and smelled of mildew and time, but there were hundreds. Mom had saved them all.

Many letters described the Rocky Mountains and great high prairies. In several, he vowed to take Mom there someday. It took twelve years to get there, and we were a foursome by the time he made good on that promise.

In 1966, when Dad was offered the scholarship for summer coursework at the University of Colorado in Boulder, we traveled almost daily. Dad would study on weekdays, but we'd go out on rides through Boulder Canyon almost every evening. On weekends, we explored the Denver Zoo or Garden of the Gods to the south or Estes Park and Rocky Mountain National Park to the north and west.

But it was the original promise of that trip that said so much about Mom and Dad as a couple. Before they were married, they were barely out of college and dirt poor. All Dad had to offer my mother was the world.

Twenty years and a million miles later, Steve and I took our turn behind the wheel en route to our grandmother's funeral in 1986. Four years later, just after we'd begun sharing an apartment in North Carolina, we returned to New England together by car right after Christmas. Such was our celebration of adulthood, brotherhood, independence, and travel at our own bidding.

I'd met my future wife Kelly at that point, but I'd argue that we weren't firmly committed until *we* followed roughly the same route five months later in May 1991. Three years after that, Steve and his future wife Lesley made the trip north. They left as friends and returned engaged.

Dad's letters to Mom in 1954 still sit in my basement, and so they shall until I move them, or they are reduced to dust themselves.

Finding perfect travel companions in love interests probably spoke more to our compatibility than anything else. If anyone could survive a ride with us across the Cross Bronx Expressway, marry 'em quick, Steve and I thought.

Be it road trips or afternoon drives, travel was a crucible for Dad, Mom, Steve, and me, out of which was forged pure gold. And so it would be with my own family—my own children. The seeds were planted early.

There's a stage in a child's life when they're old enough to dream but too young to drive; old enough to imagine mystical, enchanting places down the street or across oceans but unable to get there. Old enough to wonder but too young to wander.

At that special age, a child's mom and dad still know *everything,* princesses and dragons and castles and heroes greet you at every turn, and the scariest monsters are in closets—not out roaming the streets. Time means little, goodnight prayers and hugs and stories can go on forever, countries on the bureau-top globes are dressed up in all their primary colors like candy in a store window, and nightlights paint stars across the ceiling.

It was during this time that I made a practice of playing a game, first with my daughter Alexa and later with her younger brother Harrison. We'd sit on the bedroom carpet, and the world between us was the same dusty, outdated globe that once sat on my own shelf at their age. It had strange names written on it: "Zaire," "U.S.S.R.," and "East Germany." It also featured magical and mysterious names: "Madagascar," "Iceland," and "Zimbabwe."

"Close your eyes," I'd say, giving the globe a spin. "Now, when you're ready, put your finger down anywhere to stop it from turning."

This done, we'd discuss what life was like where their finger landed. We'd talk about how the culture was different and how wonderful it would be to go there, to see their people's beautiful faces, to taste their food, and to listen to the music of their language. Of course, fingers inevitably landed in the middle of an ocean more often than not, and the Soviet Union (as it was called on the globe) accounted for an inordinate percentage as well, but I fudged a bit. It didn't matter if I knew little about Laos and less about Lithuania.

(Once again, as with so many things, it's less important to be *right* than it is to be *sure*.)

"Canada!" I'd proclaim as they lifted their finger from somewhere on the Myanmar Peninsula. And when their finger found the U.S.S.R. for the tenth straight time, I'd shout excitedly, "Ahh, England!"

"Can we go there?" they'd ask.

"Maybe. Someday."

Once the kids reached an age where we felt they were ready for longer road trips, we purchased a family van and hit the highway. It was our habit to make a yearly pilgrimage anywhere, and driving was always cheaper than flying. We'd occasionally gone to nearby beaches or mountains, but by 2001, we'd begun undertaking classic family road trips—the kinds that stretched across states and regions and days or weeks.

Eventually, vans became SUVs and Disney theme parks became national parks. But even when they reached that age when *their* dad and mom were merely human and superheroes weren't real, and everything they learned in school on any particular day amounted to "Nuthin'... nuthin' cool," we would still put aside our prejudices and carve out a week or more together for a family trip on a grand scale.

This began what would be an annual rite for years, including numerous trips to New England, an excursion to Florida, two trips to Québec, Canada, and five trips to the American West. And we *did* visit London—we even rented a car and drove across the breadth of England, and then we rode the Chunnel to Paris.

Life is an out-and-back...or several. We rode it out for a good number of laps. This paved the way for some of the most magical and mythical experiences shared by my family. There's probably another book in that alone—another lap, *out-and-back*—for another time.

I still look forward to traveling myself. I've seen so much beauty, and there is so much more to see, so to borrow from Susan Sontag, "I haven't been everywhere, but it's on my list."

I still prescribe travel like medicine—a salve for myself and anyone else who might share the view. It continues to feed me, restore me, educate me, amaze me, and enrich me. And when I'm lost to this world, look for me somewhere on the open road. That's where I rediscovered my father. That's where I'll be found.

My children are grown now and traveling the world themselves. It's a rare and cherished occasion that I see them both in my own rearview mirror now. Having driven thousands of miles in dozens of countries, they are still spinning the globe, dropping a finger, setting a course, and cultivating memories.

Someday they may even be fortunate enough to see young impressionable passengers in their own rearview mirrors as they all gaze out together at the universe, with the stars above flying along with them.

And maybe—just maybe—they'll turn a key, roll down the windows, and sing out a song of the road:

"*Bum-bum-bo… Here we go!*"

> The things which the child loves remain
> in the domain of the heart until old age.
> The most beautiful thing in life is that our
> souls remain hovering over the places
> where we once enjoyed ourselves.
> —*Kahlil Gibran*

About the Author

Randy B. Young, a graduate of Dartmouth College, first worked as an award-winning advertising copywriter in New Hampshire. After migrating south, he worked in communications for the University of North Carolina at Chapel Hill (UNC), but he concurrently maintained an award-winning newspaper feature for twenty years and regularly wrote for regional lifestyle and sports publications. This is his first book.

After retiring from UNC, Randy has continued to write, focusing on social commentary, often ironical and always seasoned with humor. He calls Chapel Hill, North Carolina home, though he admits that he "vacationed in New England for a few decades." A self-described "child of I-95" and a lover of travel, the road has informed so many of his fond and formative memories of family as well as his writing.

Randy remains active, coaching high school track and field, teaching, and promoting a photography business. He married Kelly Maddry Young in 1992. Their daughter Alexa went to Emory University in Atlanta, earned her master's degree in public health from UNC, and lives in Charleston, South Carolina. Their son Harrison graduated from UNC and is pursuing a career in medicine at Yale University. Both children currently live many miles from Chapel Hill, but that's just another excuse for Randy, Kelly, and their lovable dog Jasper (a mysterious mix of "something spaniel-esque") to jump on I-95 and visit.

www.ingramcontent.com/pod-product-compliance
Lightning Source LLC
Chambersburg PA
CBHW030038100526
44590CB00011B/255